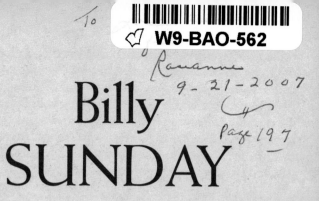

# Billy SUNDAY

## MAJOR LEAGUE EVANGELIST

### RACHAEL M. PHILLIPS

**BARBOUR**
PUBLISHING

# ACKNOWLEDGMENTS

The author would like to acknowledge the valuable help of Mr. William Darr, the director of the Grace College and Seminary Library and Archives, and his staff; Dr. Stephen Grill, curator of the Reneker Museum; Dr. William Firstenberger, Billy Sunday Museum curator; and Kim Peterson.

# ONE

John D. Rockefeller Jr., had never witnessed anything like this crusade meeting in New York City, May 1917.

The millionaire had contributed heavily to cover crusade expenses, but he waited patiently outside the "Glory Barn," Billy Sunday's massive tabernacle at 168th Street and Broadway, standing in line for hours with thousands of other people.

*Would have been nice to have reserved a seat*, thought Rockefeller. *I haven't waited in line like this for years!* But he knew, as did all Billy Sunday's acquaintances, that Billy did not grant special treatment to his friends at his revivals, even if they were wealthy and powerful.

Rockefeller finally sat down near a somewhat shabbily dressed woman with several children lined up beside her. A host of Masons occupied the section to the right. Sunday school classes, cynical reporters, white-shirted factory workers with scrubbed, black-edged fingernails, fashionably attired society women—all occupied the plain wooden benches together.

*Why am I sitting on the edge of my seat?* Rockefeller's well-honed sense of caution probed his emotions. He had helped manage his father's financial empire during much of his adult life, giving away huge sums of money to try to eradicate his "robber baron" reputation. Although raised in a religious atmosphere, he was not a man to be easily moved by revivalistic emotion. *Why is my heart beating so fast?* The very air seemed charged with electricity. Occasionally the eager hum of conversation erupted into spontaneous cheers and clapping.

Rockefeller watched as the eighteen thousand seats filled rapidly, with hundreds of people standing in the aisles. Special buses and subway trains ran every fifty seconds, bringing more and more people until thousands of hopeful crusade goers remained outside the tabernacle. Many were forced to wait until the next service.

*The huge, 344-foot-long structure resembles a giant turtle shell,* thought Rockefeller. A platform and pulpit drew his eyes to the middle of the tabernacle. Experts had designed the sounding board that hung above the pulpit and the newfangled augophones mounted in the building. The sequences of half cones carried Billy's voice to every seat. The Glory Barn, like all Billy's tabernacles, was well lit (he believed that God hated darkness) and decorated with colorful bunting and banners. Workers had spread two train carloads of red cedar sawdust on the floor; years later the fragrance of cedar would remind Rockefeller of the Sunday crusade in New York City.

"Good music," Billy Sunday had once declared, "will give the devil cold feet."[1] So the service began with more than two thousand choir members, led by Homer Rodeheaver, thundering out the strains of "Come, Thou

Almighty King," "When the Roll Is Called Up Yonder," and other hymns. Rockefeller felt as if the music had penetrated every cell of his body. After the meeting he talked to friends who had heard the powerful echoes of the songs blocks away.

Rev. Charles Goodell of St. Paul's Methodist Episcopal Church prayed, and the medium-sized, slim man on the platform behind him echoed a soft, "Oh, God, amen!" to the pastor's invocation.

The man arose and strode to the pulpit. *Billy Sunday certainly does not resemble a pastor. No Prince Albert coats for him!* Rockefeller noted with approval the perfectly cut navy suit, the silk tie, and the shiny patent-leather shoes. Billy Sunday resembled an up-and-coming businessman but also exuded the strong, confident air of the athlete he was.

Billy began his sermon quietly with the admission that he had nothing to offer but "old-time religion." Some of his supporters had worried that the metropolitan atmosphere of the enormous eastern city would intimidate the evangelist from rural Iowa. Now a few staff members on the platform exchanged glances, but he dispersed their fears in no time.

Billy had come, he told his audience, to preach the old-fashioned religion because death was a reality as old as man himself. "Man with all his genius, my friend, has never been able to change it and never will. You will die in the old-fashioned way; you will crumble to dust in the old-fashioned way." Rockefeller felt as if Billy's steely eyes were bolted to his own. "And if you are lost, you will go to old-fashioned hell!" he thundered. His words slammed into his listeners like shrapnel.

Billy paused. Slowly, deliberately, he climbed down

from the platform and stood so close the brave souls in the front rows could see tiny beads of sweat seeping from his forehead.

"But if you are saved. . . ," he said softly.

Rockefeller did not realize he was holding his breath.

"If you are saved," Billy's voice rose, "it will be in the old-fashioned way. The way of the cross leads home. And by the old-fashioned religion of your father and your mother, oh, New York!" he roared.

Billy preached for almost two hours. No one left, despite the fact that most in the congregation would face a regular workday the next morning. His listeners' attention did not drift as the night wore on. Instead, Billy pulled them to him by invisible cords that grew tauter with every sentence. Even the most disdainful journalist found himself leaning forward to hear the evangelist. Finally, Billy invited the people to ask Jesus Christ to change their lives.

"Whosoever will may come. If God Almighty would send an angel down to this old world to tell it of His love, he'd have to stop every thief on the street and say, 'God so loved the world,' he'd go into Sing Sing and into the debt house and say, 'God so loved the world,' he'd go down, my friends, to the White Way, into every theater and every cabaret, he'd say to them, wild, wayward, crowding to perdition, drinking, cursing, blaspheming, 'God so loved the world.' He'd go into every haunt of vice and sin, he'd stop every girl on the street, my friend, he'd go to the haunts of vice and say that 'God so loved the world.' " The evangelist paced and pointed as he talked.

"He'd go to the East side, he'd go in every nook and corner of the city, he'd go down Fifth Avenue, down Broadway, he'd go into the great newspapers and say,

'God so loved the world.' He'd walk up and down Wall Street and cry it in the stock exchange, he'd go, my friends, into the great banks and cry it. He'd stand in front of Trinity and cry it to the surging crowds down the street, and he'd cry out, and he'd go up and down the land unless there might be some sinner, somewhere, that angel wouldn't find."

Billy had scaled his pulpit as if it were a mountain. He stood high above the crowd and threw his arms open wide, his face shining with passion. "God has emblazoned it on His Word that He so loved the world that He gave His only begotten Son that whosoever believed in Him might not perish but have everlasting life." He waited for a moment as if listening, then slowly climbed down. His voice dropped so low the congregation strained to hear him.

"I can't preach it any better. Well, Jesus, I don't know any more to say. . . . I don't know, Lord. . .the words which would even begin to tell this crowd how much God loves them, what His love wants to do for them.

"Thank you, Lord—and say, Lord, help them here by the hundreds to come down and say, 'Well, I will tell you, I am a big chump to live in rebellion against a God like that, a God that loves me and did all that for me. . . .' "[2]

God answered Billy Sunday's prayer with a surge of men, women, boys, and girls who flooded the aisles of the tabernacle like the Atlantic at high tide. Before the crusade ended in June, more than one hundred thousand people responded to Billy's appeals.

Rockefeller leaped to his feet and rushed to shake Billy's hand at the end of the service. Billy had once referred to Rockefeller's immensely wealthy father as "the hungriest man in all the world."[3] John Rockefeller Jr., felt as if he would burst from all he had taken in, yet he longed to hear more. *Am I as "hungry" as my father? How can a farm boy from Iowa affect me this way?*

Thousands of Billy Sunday crusade goers had asked themselves the same question.

Billy Sunday was born in a two-room log cabin near Ames, Iowa, on November 19, 1862. His mother, Jennie, held her baby boy, thankful to have finished labor and delivery once more. *Died Nov. 6 1935 pg. 201*

"Willie," she murmured, pressing her lips on his soft baby hair. Willie's father, a newly enlisted soldier in the Union Army, had written his wife from military camp, requesting that they name the baby after him, if it was a boy. "William Ashley Sunday," said the new mother proudly. How on earth had William thought of the name Ashley? Certainly no one in his German background carried that name.

Tiny Willie cried weakly, and his mother stroked him anxiously and held him to her breast. The baby, who later became "Billy," was much smaller than her other sons had been at birth, and he had difficulty nursing.

"Oh, dear Lord, give me strength," prayed Jennie wearily. Her mother was caring for four-year-old Albert and two-year-old Howard Edwin for a few days. Kind neighbors had brought in what food they could spare, but Jennie knew she would struggle during the months ahead, especially without William.

"But we'll hear from him soon," Jennie told the whimpering baby, rubbing his back. "Your pa will send us a letter, and we'll be able to buy cornmeal and bacon and maybe some Christmas candy for the big boys." Jennie and William had both hoped his enlistment would guarantee a steady, if small, income, and their desperate financial situation would improve.

"I'll take good care of you, Willie," she promised. "When your pa comes home, you'll be big and strong. He'll be so proud of his boys!"

A letter did arrive a few days later. Humming to herself, Jennie read it once more before she went to bed alone on the straw tick in the corner of the main room. Today she had bought two striped peppermint sticks for the pair of ragged little stockings to be hung from the mantel. The boys' grandparents would give them each an orange for Christmas, she knew.

"The only time you two are still is when you're asleep," she whispered to the quiet little boys in the trundle bed.

She picked up Willie from his cradle. *I'll try to feed him again, now that things have settled down.* Worry tried to wrap itself around her like a smothering quilt. Willie often fretted and fussed, and his brothers' raucous presence made it almost impossible to nurse him. But now the baby snuggled close to his mother, and Jennie smiled to see him eat.

*Thank you, Lord, for all my blessings. Even though William is away, we'll have a merry Christmas.*

The Sunday family did have a wonderful Christmas at Jennie's parents' nearby house. Her mother brought in a ham from the smokehouse and baked a wild turkey and many kinds of pie. Even "Squire" Martin Corey, her stern father, seemed to understand that his daughter and her children needed a little extra support with William gone. He allowed the boys to try on his coonskin cap. He wrestled with them and charged through the house with his grandsons on his back while their grandmother and mother put dinner on the table.

Jennie smiled at him gratefully, and the squire touched her shoulder awkwardly. She brought Willie in on the pillow that seemed to soothe his colic better than anything else. Jennie calmed her noisy sons for prayer, then enjoyed watching them stuff themselves like little piglets.

Jennie knew her mother would send the remainder of the feast home with them in a picnic basket. They would eat well for a few weeks or more. Then, surely, another letter would arrive from William. He would send money to feed them all and gentle words to ease her longing.

A letter did arrive from Camp Patterson, Missouri, later that winter, but an unfamiliar hand had written the address.

William was dead.

He had marched with his company through the raw December weather across the Iron Mountains. Lack of sanitation and poor medical care in the camp devastated William, who probably caught a dangerous form of measles. Like many soldiers in the Union and Confederate armies, he died before he ever fired a shot in battle.

A box of William's personal effects arrived not long after the letter. It contained his clothing, a few official documents, and ten cents.

*He'll never play his fiddle for me again.* Tears streamed down Jennie's cheeks as she tried to patch little shirts that already had been mended several times. *Even Albert may not remember you, Will. How can your own boys not remember you?*

Baby Willie woke up fussing, as he always did. Jennie picked him up mechanically, her tears falling on his coarse little shirt.

*Now he'll never see you, Willie. You'll never grab his thick, soft beard like your brothers did. . . .*

Numbly, Jennie mixed corn bread that evening, wiped dirty faces, washed the thick, chipped dishes. She could not think of explaining William's death to the boys or planning for the future.

For now, breathing seemed work enough.

"Albert! Ed! Keep Willie from getting underfoot while I fix supper!" chided Jennie.

"Ma, we want to go outside!" protested Albert. The boys wanted to see the barn cat's new kittens.

Jennie's ears detected the sound of approaching wagon wheels. Her father and mother had been working down at the sugar shed, tending the fires so the temperature would remain constant, stirring the sap as it boiled, skimming the impurities as they rose to the top. Squire Corey, never patient during the year and a half they had lived with her folks, was even less so when he was famished. Supper was only half-prepared because Willie had clung to her skirts possessively all afternoon.

*Would it be better for Pa to come home to the noise of all three boys inside or just Willie screaming because he couldn't go with the others?*

"Go," Jennie said shortly to Albert. He and Ed exploded out the door as Willie let out a thin wail that seemed to grow higher and louder every minute.

*How can such a puny child make all that noise?* Jennie shifted the scrawny two-year-old to her hip and clattered around the kitchen, trying to make up for lost time.

By nightfall, Jennie felt as if her very soul had drained out that day. Squire Corey had been greeted by a hysterical Albert and Ed, whom the cat had scratched when they tried to hold her offspring. He ate crunchy beans and burned biscuits for supper, to the accompaniment of Willie's incessant sirenlike whine and the older boys' constant jostling. Jennie's mother had tried to soothe everyone, despite her own exhaustion, but the evening had ended with Squire Corey giving both Albert and Ed a whipping with his razor strap and sending them to bed. How many times had this happened? Jennie had lost count.

*Moving in with Pa and Ma was the only way to feed my boys and keep the farm,* Jennie thought, nestling into the soft feather bed. She loved it, but she had slept better on the old straw ticks back in the cabin. *I just don't know if we can do it any more. There has to be some other way.*

A man's face rose in her mind, a face she had seen at church the past several weeks. The dark eyes looked at her approvingly, just as they had when the Coreys and Jennie and her brood had filed past the solitary man into their usual pew.

*Some other way.*

# TWO

"Ma, we want to go to Grandpa's."

Jennie looked into two sets of eager eyes and sighed. Would Squire Corey welcome Ed and Willie today or brusquely send them away the minute they set foot in his yard?

"Let 'em go," said Leroy. Jennie felt a quick, hot wave of resentment toward her husband of six years. *Please help me, Lord.* She forced herself to smile and said, "Well, it's a mighty fine day, and your grandpa could probably use some help with the garden."

Eight-year-old Willie tore across the pasture, easily beating his older brother. Jennie left her husband to brood by himself in the cabin. She put more wood on the fire in the front yard and stirred the boiling water in the big black laundry kettle. Who would have thought that such a tiny, weak baby could have grown into such an active boy? Fearful that he would die before he reached school age, Jennie had consulted an old French doctor, who had administered some herbs to the three-year-old. Willie improved rapidly and was soon outracing the entire neighborhood. Now it was all Jennie could do to keep sight of him.

Willie had started attending the little, one-room, neighborhood school the past fall, which at least kept him from antagonizing Leroy during the day. But spring had arrived. Willie spent every spare minute he could on his grandfather's farm. *The boys really are a help, at times,* Jennie reminded herself. They helped the squire build fences, chop wood, and take care of the animals. *I know he would never say it, but I think they keep him company, too.* She grinned and breathed a prayer of thanksgiving that Willie and Ed were such healthy, energetic little boys. She needed their vitality just to keep going. If only the others. . . Jennie tried to hold back her tears, knowing that Leroy did not like to hear her cry.

She had hoped so much to create a new life for herself and her children when she married Leroy Heizer, the emigrant from Indiana who had smiled so pleasantly at Jennie at church. She thought Leroy was an answer to her prayers.

Much had gone wrong almost immediately. Albert had been kicked by a horse; now he fell into convulsions almost every day. He seemed less and less aware of what was going on around him and sometimes exploded into tantrums that enraged his stepfather, who demanded Albert be sent to an asylum.

Jennie had become pregnant almost immediately with Leroy Jr., then Libbie.

*Libbie. . .* Jennie could not squelch the sob that fought its way out of her throat. She banged the kettle lid so Leroy would not notice, but she could not stop grieving for her only daughter, her precious little toddler whose dress had caught fire. Libbie had died of her burns.

Perhaps their marriage would not have gone so badly if misfortune had not darkened every moment. The overwhelmed Leroy had begun to drink excessively, and instead of a husband, Jennie felt as if she had to care for one more dependent child. Sometimes she wondered where the family would get its next meal.

Jennie had believed Leroy would father her boys, making up for the loss of William, but no warmth had developed between them. She remembered the first time her husband had stumbled home in the middle of the night, so drunk he could not open the door by himself.

*I shouldn't let him in when he's like that. . . .*

"You and Ed take this cornmeal up to your ma's house," commanded Squire Corey. "I'll carry the meat."

Willie and Ed exchanged glad smiles. Lugging the heavy bag across the fields was hard work, but the bulging white cotton sack meant hot, steaming corn-bread for dinner. Leroy had not worked much the past several weeks, and Billy's shrunken stomach craved a full meal.

*Lazy, good-for-nothin' bum,* thought Willie as he and Ed carried the cornmeal. As he grew older, Willie had realized his stepfather's "sickness" usually occurred after his bouts of drinking. *Why did Ma have to marry him? We were getting along fine until he came.*

Although he had been quite small when the marriage took place, Willie vividly remembered the resentment he felt when he had to move from his grandparents' comfortable farmhouse to the dark, ramshackle cabin. He and his brothers no longer ate savory ham and bacon from his grandfather's smokehouse every day or the squirrel and rabbit the squire hunted each week. Instead, they subsisted on porridge and whatever else their mother could scrape together.

Worst of all, Leroy seemed to fill the cabin with his dark presence. When Willie awoke to greet the sunshine, he, Ed, and Albert had to keep quiet so they would not annoy their stepfather. Jennie gave Leroy the biggest plate of food at every meal. Willie could hardly bear to see his stepfather hold Jennie's hand or touch her face. When Leroy and Jennie stood close together, Willie wriggled between them and clung to his mother's skirts. Much of the time he stayed with his grandmother. She welcomed her rowdy grandchildren and brightened their days with good food and fun.

But she had died not long afterward. *I miss Grandma so much*, thought Willie as he trudged on. *If she were alive now, we'd be carrying one of her pies, too.*

As the cabin came into view, Willie hoped that Leroy's hangover had overcome him. Maybe he had gone back to bed to sleep all day. Then Jennie and the boys could have some peace. Billy's blue eyes hardened as he remembered the first time the family had encountered Leroy's alcohol problem.

Loud, raucous swearing had awakened four-year-old Willie from a deep sleep.

"It's the bogeyman!" Ed whispered. "He's gonna eat us all!" He dove under the trundle bed quilts.

But Willie recognized the tall, lanky frame leaning on his mother. It was Leroy.

"Get away from my ma!" he shouted. "Get away!"

Billy jumped out of bed and began whacking the intruder with his small fists, only to be swatted aside like a fly by Leroy's big hand. The preschooler bloodied his nose on the old chest at the foot of Jennie's bed, but he attacked again.

"Willie! No!" Jennie cried. Fearing Willie would bite her husband, as he sometimes did his brothers, she grabbed her son and huddled with him in a corner as Leroy ranted and raved. Willie could still feel his mother's tight, bony arms around him, the flutter of her terrified heart, the thudding of his own tiny one. Leroy had collapsed on the big bed, but Jennie had not moved until his snores reverberated throughout the cabin.

During the past year, Leroy's drunken rages had worsened in frequency and intensity. Willie and his brothers now slept in the loft, so they found it easier to avoid their stepfather when he was intoxicated. But the boys worried about their mother when they heard Leroy's unsure steps approaching the house.

"Ma, are you all right?" they would call down to Jennie. "Ma?"

Billy gritted his teeth as he carried the cornmeal the last few yards. *Wish we could keep this bag up in the loft and throw it down on Pa when he gets so crazy.*

To his relief, he saw only Jennie and Leroy Jr., in the front yard.

At first Billy detected panic on his mother's face. The squire did not usually accompany his grandsons home.

*Oh, Lord, what did they do this time?* Jennie thought. But her face broke into a smile when she saw the food they carried. *Oh, God, You knew the cupboards were empty. You knew. Thank You, thank You, Lord!*

Willie and Ed grunted mightily as they triumphantly brought the cornmeal to their mother. The squire followed, carrying dried venison and a large ham.

"Thought you could use this," said her father gruffly.

"Thanks," said Jennie, knowing Pa hated demonstrativeness of any kind.

"Go get washed up," he ordered Willie and Ed, and the two went inside.

"Your Willie—" the squire paused.

"Yes?" Jennie held her breath. Had her mischievous son let the cows out of the pasture again?

"Willie and me was pulling weeds in the garden. He didn't say much, even though Willie usually makes more noise than the blue jays jabberin'. After a while he sat down under a currant bush and did nothin' at all."

This was akin to unforgivable sin. Jennie could not believe her father's measured tone.

"He was thinkin', I could tell, so I pulled weeds by myself for a while. Then I said, 'Willie, what you got on your mind?'" An unmistakable twinkle appeared in Squire Corey's eyes under his wild, thick, gray eyebrows. "He told me, 'I think I'm not going to pull weeds when I get to be a man. I'm going to hunt around and find a good job I can work at with my head.'"[1]

Willie would pull many weeds and do much heavy farm work before baseball and his crusade career made his dreams come true. Neighboring farmers sometimes employed Willie and Ed when they were not busy helping their grandfather. Willie guided the lead horse of a team pulling a reaper during a wheat harvest, earning twenty-five cents per day. The drudgery of endless burning sun and aching exhaustion evaporated when the youngster spent his entire earnings of two dollars to enlarge and frame a tiny portrait of his little half sister, Libbie, whom he missed deeply.

Willie's childhood did not consist solely of hard times

and disappointments. He learned much from his grandfather, helping him construct wagons, houses, stone walls,
waterwheels, looms, and a cane mill. The squire even
taught Willie acrobatics. He learned so well to ride standing on a horse's bare back that a visiting circus wanted to
employ him.

Willie and Ed were inseparable, working together,
playing together, and getting in trouble together, most
often at school and church.

"Ed, Willie," said his mother in exasperation, "why
can't you sit still in Sunday school?" Jennie took her
family to a little log-cabin church each week. "Miss Sel-
lars tells me she had to stand you both in the corner
again." *If only Leroy would come with me to church!* Fraz-
zled and weary, Jennie shushed a whining Leroy Jr., and
tried to persuade Albert to stay still in the wagon as she
drove home from church without her husband.

"Does Grandpa know?" asked Ed anxiously. He
knew this would mean another session with the squire's
razor strap.

"No, he does not know. But I will tell him if it will
make you listen. Don't you boys know that loving God
is more important than anything?"

Her voice rose and almost cracked.

Ed and Willie stared at their mother with round
eyes. Jennie rarely raised her voice.

Finally Willie said, "Yes, Ma. We know loving God
is important."

They did. Even when their mother faced days of
want and exhaustion, Jennie sang hymns as she worked
and prayed with her children at bedtime.

Her Christian faith had sustained her through years
of toil and disappointment. Jennie would need every

prayer, every word from the Bible she knew to help her through the difficult times ahead.

"Ed. Willie. I need to talk to you both."

Willie mentally calculated his sins of the past week. He and Ed had harassed their teacher until the tired woman had dismissed school early on Friday. He had won several fights after school, gone swimming in a forbidden creek even though it was still chilly, and tormented Leroy more than usual. Grandpa had banished the brothers from his farm because he said they were lazy and worthless. Worst of all, he and Ed stole their classmates' lunches and often pilfered crackers from the general store barrel when Mr. Bonhoeffer was busy with another customer. But they had been so hungry. . . .

Jennie showed no signs of anger. She hugged Ed and Willie and began to weep, her tears soaking their hair.

"Ma! Ma!" Willie could not bear it. *Ma cried like this when Pa left for good last year. But I thought things were all better, now that he's gone.*

"We're sorry, Ma!" Willie mentally promised that he would steal only when he was *very* hungry.

Jennie ignored the near-confession and tried to quench her tears.

"Ed, Willie. Since your pa has been gone, things have gotten worse and worse. I have only a little money left, maybe enough to put you boys on the train to the Soldiers' Home in Glenwood."

"Soldiers' Home? But this is our home."

Jennie began to weep again, and the boys clung to her, tears starting to roll down their cheeks.

"They will take good care of you." Jennie tried to reassure herself as well as Ed and Willie. *Maybe they can keep you out of trouble. The Lord knows you're getting too big for me to handle.* "You'll have enough to eat, and clothes, and schooling. You aren't learning much here."

The boys knew that was true. Together they had managed to disrupt the school most of the time.

But now Ed, who at eleven was as tall as his mother, and nine-year-old Willie, who intimidated boys several years older with his fearless love of fighting, cried like little children.

"But, Ma, I don't want to be away from you. We're not orphans! Why are you sending us to an orphans' home? Why, Ma? Why?"

# THREE

Waiting. Waiting.

The dark, raw night did not seem like spring, Willie thought. But then, at one o'clock in the morning, he was always snuggled in his quilts beside Ed in the loft at home. He hated this empty waiting. It reminded him of the night after Libbie had been buried, when he had sneaked out to the graveyard to be with her so she wouldn't be afraid of the dark. Now Jennie, Willie, and Ed stood outside the little hotel in Ames, Iowa, in the faint light from the one kerosene lamp at the hotel desk, slipping inside only to warm themselves when the cold air chilled them to their bones.

"Did I hear the train whistle?" asked Willie.

His mother nodded and burst into a fresh paroxysm of weeping. The frightened boys huddled close to her, and she gripped them tightly. The few other waiting travelers carefully skirted the little group, looking away to the black horizon. A streak of gray lightened the darkness, then the powerful locomotive rumbled into the small town, breathing fire and steam like a dragon.

With trembling fingers, Jennie pinned a note on each boy's ragged coat.

"Ma, I don't need any silly note!" protested Ed. "I'm eleven years old! I can remember where we're going."

"I can, too!" echoed Willie.

Their mother smiled through her tears. "You are smart boys; I know that. Well, you can put them in your pockets, along with the letter to the Soldiers' Home and your tickets to Council Bluffs."

"Council Bluffs? But Ma, ain't the Soldiers' Home in Glenwood?"

Jennie paused, her face quivering. "Yes, it is," she said painfully. "But I only had enough money to get you to Council Bluffs. God is going to have to get you the rest of the way!" She fought the sobs that tried to swallow her breath. "Ed and Willie, be good boys. You must say your prayers every night. I will pray, too. . . ." She gave them a final hug, touched their wet faces, then gently pushed them toward the train door, where the conductor made his last call for passengers.

Willie charged blindly onto the train. He and Ed waved frantically from a window. Jennie tried to smile bravely as the train pulled away from the only home the boys had ever known. They would not see their mother again for four long years.

Farms, fences, and silent little towns with only a few shining lights flew past the window as if they were racing the train through the night. At any other time, the boys would have been glued to the scenery, trying to pierce the darkness to spot each new sight. But the novelty of riding a train for the first time did not overcome the boys' grief. Willie cried until his eyes felt empty. Ed sniffled and sobbed. The other passengers had seated themselves as far away from the two weeping children as they could.

"Ed, I'm hungry."

"I know, Willie. I am, too. You know Ma didn't have nothin' to send with us."

*That's why we're here, ridin' this train to an orphans' home. Ma can't feed us, and Grandpa won't.* Willie's resentment filled his empty stomach and fermented there. *Don't do any good to sit and think about it. May as well try to sleep.*

The children huddled close together and slept deeply. Although the train lurched as it made its regular stops and starts through the countryside, Willie and Ed heard nothing until the conductor woke them and informed the boys that the next stop was Council Bluffs. They would have to get off the train.

"Wisht I was home," grumbled Ed.

"So do I, but we ain't, so let's try to find something to eat." Willie trudged wearily toward the town in the morning sunshine. *At least it ain't raining,* he thought.

Delicious fragrances of frying bacon and eggs drifting from the back of the hotel near the train tracks set his shriveled stomach aquiver.

"Let's go check the garbage," said Ed eagerly. The boys ran behind the building and began to rummage through the trash.

"Nothin' good! Just a bunch of old shredded socks!"

Willie thought he would bawl like a baby. But he said, "Ed, these socks would make a good sock ball, and we could play some catch."

The boys rolled and tied until a knobby, shapeless ball materialized. Ed tossed it to Willie, who caught it easily. *Now I know Ed's hungry. He always throws a ball hard enough to hurt.* He threw it back.

"Let's throw it over the shed!" Ed tossed the sock ball on the peaked roof of a nearby shed, and Willie dashed to the other side to catch it. The boys ran and shouted, forgetting where they were until a woman's unfriendly face appeared at the back door of the hotel.

"You young 'uns go on home now!"

Willie clutched the ball in one hand. His knees trembled under him.

"We can't go home. Our ma put us on the train."

"On the train? Are you boys going to visit your kin?"

"No, ma'am," answered Ed. "We ain't got no place to go unless we make it to the Soldiers' Home in Glenwood."

The woman's flinty gray eyes suddenly softened. "You boys lose your pa in the war?" she asked gently.

They nodded. "Our real pa died in the war, and our other pa left," said Ed.

Willie gulped longingly. The breakfast smells that poured from the open doorway were almost too much for him to bear.

"Come on in, then," she said. "S'pose you ain't had nothin' to eat. You'll wash dishes and scrub pots, but I ain't never gonna turn away soldiers' young 'uns."

Willie ate biscuit after biscuit spread with melting butter and wild strawberry preserves. Ed attacked the flapjacks as if they were an enemy. The two demolished a platter of eggs. The woman even gave them a piece of sausage each, saying, "Sausage's for the guests, but Charles would have wanted you to have it."

"Who's Charles?" asked Ed.

27

"Charles Hampton was my husband." Mrs. Hampton turned away and stoked the fire. "He was killed at Gettysburg."

"I'll go get you some more wood," said Willie. He wiped his mouth on his sleeve and headed out the back door with Ed at his heels. The two brought in wood until Mrs. Hampton declared she could burn the hotel down with what they had hauled. They washed piles of dirty dishes without complaint, although Willie particularly despised kitchen chores. Mrs. Hampton let the tired boys nap beside the fireplace, then handed them big bowls of beans and corn bread.

"We gotta go now, Mrs. Hampton," said Ed after they had cleaned up the noontime dishes.

*Where? Where are we going?* thought Willie. But he held his hat in his hands as Ma had taught him. They both thanked the woman for her kindness. She pressed a bag of corn bread into their hands and watched as the boys walked toward the railroad tracks.

*She wa'n't no beauty,* thought Willie, *but Ma says God sometimes sends angels that look like everybody else. Maybe Mrs. Hampton was our angel.* Aloud he said, "All right, Mr. Know-It-All, do you know where we're goin'?"

"Sure," said Ed. "I got a plan." He gestured with his head. "I heard somebody in the dining room say the next train to Glenwood leaves at two thirty. We gotta sneak onto that train."

Willie's eyes lit up. With his full stomach, he was ready for any adventure that came his way.

The brothers slipped to the far end of the train station and flattened themselves against the wall. Ed peered cautiously toward the tracks.

"We're in luck, Willie."

"Why do you say that, Ed?"

" 'Cause there's a couple of ladies with young 'uns waitin' for the train."

"Why is *that* good luck?"

"Don't you see, if we stand with them, the conductor'll think we're their boys. Maybe we can get on the train and make it to Glenwood afore he finds out we're not."

Willie nodded in admiration at Ed's scheme. "Let's go!"

"Don't stand *too* close to them," Ed cautioned in a whisper. He and Willie wandered casually toward the groups. They played an impromptu game of tag. Soon two of the waiting children joined in their fun.

When the tall conductor called, "All aboard!" he saw two businessmen, an elderly lady, and two mothers with flocks of children. One had a baby, he noticed with displeasure. Crying, noise, smelly diapers—he was glad it would not be a long journey.

Willie and Ed followed the women and children into the railroad car and sat in front of the lady who carried the baby. The train gave a slow lurch like a tired hound dog and reluctantly pulled out of the station.

"Riding a train is a lot more fun during the day," Willie told Ed as the engine gathered speed. The flying farmhouses and fence posts outside the train windows fascinated him. The farm animals in the fields seemed drawn backwards by a giant magnet. Willie almost forgot that he and Ed had entered the train without paying.

But soon the tall conductor entered the car, and the boys froze.

"Tickets, ma'am," he said to the mothers, and they both handed their tickets to him.

"But these aren't enough, ma'am," said the conductor to the lady behind Willie and Ed. "Them boys are too big to go on the train for free."

"But they're not my children!" She stared at him indignantly.

The conductor gestured to the other woman, and she, too, glared at the confused man.

He scowled at the boys. "Tickets, *now*."

They gazed at him with blank terror.

"You boys thinkin' you'd go for a little joy ride?"

"N—no, sir," answered Willie. "We're just tryin' to get to Glenwood."

"Well, you can go there if you can pay for a ticket."

"Don't have any money, sir."

"Then I'll just throw the both of you off by the seat of your pants. Maybe I'll wait till the train gets goin' *real* fast. *Then* I'll throw you off."

The boys' eyes widened in horror. "Please, please, sir," begged Ed. "We just want to get to the Soldiers' Home. Our ma can't feed us, and she tried to send us there. She only had enough money to get us as far as Council Bluffs."

The big man's eyes glistened, but he said roughly, "How do I know you two ain't runnin' away from home 'cause your pappy whaled the tar out of you?"

"I got a letter from my ma, sir, to the head of the Soldiers' Home. Look."

"Our pa can't whale the tar out of us," said Willie. "He died in the war."

The conductor held the letter close to his near-sighted eyes. *Maybe he'll see we're not tryin' to run away and let us off at the next stop,* thought Willie. *But then what will we do?*

The conductor blew his nose loudly and cleared his

throat. "You boys sit there and behave yourselves for the rest of the trip. I'll see that you get to the Soldiers' Home in Glenwood myself."

The floor matron, Mrs. Ellen Stoltz, shushed Willie and Ed as they entered the huge room full of sleeping boys. The orphanage seemed like a mansion to the new arrivals, compared to their cabin in Ames. To their relief, the matron found them beds next to each other.

Billy did not close his eyes until after the hall clock struck midnight. A loud, tolling bell roused him from a deep sleep the next morning.

"Wash up for breakfast," Mrs. Stoltz instructed them. To their staring roommates, she snapped, "The rest of you go downstairs at once. You'll have plenty of time to meet the new boys later."

Willie noticed they wasted no time in doing as she said. He and Ed walked slowly down to the dining hall. Rows of tables and chairs filled the room. Sixty children of all sizes entered in lines and stood behind their chairs quietly while the director intoned a solemn blessing on the meal.

Willie and Ed were directed to a table of boys their age, all devouring big bowls of mush. "The food'll be better later," whispered the freckled, snaggletoothed boy across from Ed. Sure enough, Willie and Ed found themselves eating a noontime dinner of boiled ham, wilted lettuce, peas, biscuits, and rhubarb pudding with cream. The brothers took full advantage of the best spread of food they had seen since Christmas.

The same boy grinned at them. "Good, huh?"

Billy nodded emphatically as he stuffed himself. *Maybe we'll be friends.* For the first time, Willie

31

considered the possibility that life at the orphanage might be positive. As time went on, he began to see Ma had been right about some things. When Willie got up each morning, he knew breakfast awaited him, and dinner and supper, too. Willie now wore a pair of pants that fit him and a clean shirt. When the weather grew cold, he was given warm shoes and socks and a coat that did not let in the freezing north wind.

Willie loved playing in the forests that surrounded the Soldiers' Home. He learned to hunt rabbits and squirrels with Ed and the other boys. The orphanage often organized races and games for the children, and Willie won many prizes, as well as the admiration of the other orphans. His gift for oratory also caught the attention of the entire home. When Willie Sunday was to "speak a piece," the children, as well as the teachers, knew his energy and boundless enthusiasm would make it the most exciting they had ever heard.

But that did not keep him from missing his ma and little half brother, Leroy. Sometimes he was so homesick, he could hardly sleep.

Willie was accustomed to heavy farm work and did not mind his daily chores too much. But he chafed against the strict rules the director and matrons enforced. He and Ed both hated school. They tried to disrupt their classes as they had in Ames, and the director whipped them both and restricted them to bread and milk for a week. Willie could take the whipping—though it was the hardest he had received since his stepfather lived at home—but he could not bear watching the other children feast on fried chicken and apple pie while he and Ed ate cold biscuits. Willie learned to sit still.

Sabbath Days were always the worst. Dressed in

their uncomfortable Sunday best, the children had to endure a two-hour sermon, memorizing the text to repeat later. They were not allowed to play outside but had to read or study or pray. Willie thought he would die from slow suffocation on Sundays.

Still, Willie often managed to create a little excitement. He had not lived at Glenwood long before he encountered Herbert Sanford, a beefy twelve-year-old who enjoyed tormenting those smaller than himself. When the Sunday boys arrived at the orphanage, Herbie did not attempt to initiate them with his usual thrashing. After all, Willie and Ed stuck together most of the time. Herbie was smart enough to restrict his bullying to situations he could handle. But when he threw little Freddy Green's "teddy bear," an old sock with a face drawn on it, into the pond, Freddy kept all the boys awake several nights in a row with his crying. The Sunday brothers and several of the other dormitory boys met behind the barn to discuss the situation.

"Let's drag ol' Herbie out in the middle of the night and dunk him in the horse tank," suggested Rob Carson, a wiry, black-haired twelve-year-old.

"Let's do it! Drown the rat!" the boys cheered.

"But if we drag 'im out, Matron will hear us, and we'll all get a whipping," cautioned Ed.

"Well, how are we gonna get Herbie out, then? Tap him on the shoulder and say, 'Excuse me, Mr. Sanford, would you like an ice-cold bath?' "

Gerald Sutton, the snaggletoothed boy who had first welcomed the Sundays, minced across the barnyard in a too-faithful imitation of Mrs. Pratt, the wife of the orphanage's main benefactor. The boys collapsed in laughter until Ed told them to quiet down before somebody heard their secret meeting.

"Ain't no way we can drag Herbie down to the horse tank or anywhere else," said Ed. "He won't come with us unless he wants to come."

"Why would he want to come?" asked Grant Sawyer.

"He likes to fight kids who are younger than him," said Willie. "He'd come for a fight."

"But who would fight him?" Grant had to know all the answers.

"I would," said Willie. His blue eyes glinted.

"Hurray for Willie Sunday! Hurray!" The boys threw their caps in the air in celebration of the upcoming event.

"Shh!" Ed held a finger to his lips. "You want Matron to hear us?"

The boys then whispered their plans. Rob, Ed, and Willie would challenge Herbie to the fight. They would all slip out of bed when the hall clock struck three Saturday morning. Mrs. Sally Macon, a grandmotherly lady who relieved their usual suspicious matron, Mrs. Stoltz, on Friday nights was hard of hearing. The boys could sneak out to a grove of trees about a quarter mile from the school. They swore each other to secrecy, solemnly pricking their fingers to sign their initials in blood on the paper Ed had brought.

"You think you can take 'im?" Ed asked Willie later when they dried dishes alone in the kitchen. "He's bigger than you, you know."

"Sure." Willie's face showed no sign of fear. In fact, he looked as if he were looking forward to the fight. Ed said no more, privately resolving to pound Herbie Sanford's face into a pulp if he hurt his brother.

"Get 'im, Willie!"

"Bash his face in!"

A dozen boys gathered, their eyes glowing in the kerosene lantern light.

Willie danced around a little, jabbing fiercely at the air. Herbie held up a large piece of kindling and balanced it on his shoulder.

"Knock it off, you little sissy." A scornful smile split his heavy face.

In a moment, Willie streaked for his opponent and flipped the chip several feet away, landing a hard blow on Herbie's shoulder in the process.

The smile turned into a snarl, and Herbie extended his powerful hands to grab the little fighter, who seemed to buzz in and out of his grasp like a mosquito.

"That's it, Willie!"

"Get 'im!"

"Don't let 'im touch you!"

Herbie jabbed and grabbed at the infuriating Willie, but wounded only the air. Willie danced and skittered like a water bug, landing punch after punch on the bully's face. Herbie lumbered and roared like a blinded bear, but he could only connect occasionally before the fast, wiry Willie escaped him once more. As the fight went on, the late hour and Willie's speed wore the big boy down. He began to weave and stumble, and the boys' triumphant shouts echoed through the woods when Willie finally knocked Herbie to the cold ground. Willie pounded the older boy mercilessly until Ed and Rob dragged him away from the whimpering bully.

"You gonna pick on little kids anymore, Herbie?" Willie wiped blood from his upper lip. "Or you want some more?"

"N–no, I don't want no more." Herbie lurched to his feet, his face a mass of bruises, blood, and tears.

"Tell anyone who did this, and we'll all give it to you," said Ed.

Herbie glanced from one grim face to another and nodded.

"Now, let's get back to school afore anybody misses us."

They washed the two fighters' faces in the pond, then stealthily made their way back up the drainpipes and through the windows to their dormitory, where Mrs. Macon snored peacefully. The next day, after the matron cared for Herbie's injuries, the school director questioned him, but he steadfastly refused to identify his fellow combatant. The director then restricted Herbie to corn bread and milk for the rest of the week.

*Don't think he'll give in*, thought Willie, munching his thick, chunky sugar cookies at dinner the next day. *I don't think he'll tell who beat him up.*

Somehow the cookies did not taste as good as usual.

That night when Herbie turned the covers down on his bed, he found a small cloth-wrapped package there. It contained a big sugar cookie.

The matrons and teachers observed Herbie's new attitude toward the other children and privately blessed whoever had produced the change. Now that Herbie had given up bullying small children, he had more time to play games with the other boys. While Willie and Herbie never became best friends, Herbie did teach Willie a better ball-throwing technique. A few other troublemakers took note of Herbie's reform and decided to avoid future incidents.

Nobody wanted another lesson from Willie Sunday.

# FOUR

W hy can't we stay here? Why are they sending us away?"

"They're closing Glenwood, Billy. We gotta go to the Soldiers' Home in Davenport," said Ed.

"Davenport! That's clear across the state!" Billy had grown during his year-and-a-half stay in Glenwood. He had even changed his nickname because "Willie" sounded too juvenile. Even though he was now almost eleven, Billy fought back tears. Good-byes, train trips to strange places—it sounded too much like their first journey away from Ma. Sudden panic seized him. "We're goin' together to Davenport, aren't we?"

Ed smiled. "Sure, we are," he answered. "The whole orphanage has to go."

When the boys, along with the sixty other Glenwood orphans, climbed aboard the train, Billy had to admit this trip was starting much better than the other had. A familiar face greeted them: their old friend, the conductor. After their first encounter in Council Bluffs, he had returned numerous times to the Soldiers' Home in Glenwood to visit Ed and Billy, bringing them bags of peanuts or sticks of horehound candy. Now he patted their shoulders reassuringly.

"How long afore we get to Davenport?" asked Ed.

"A long time," said the conductor. "We take this here Burlington train to Des Moines, then the Rock Island to Davenport."

Des Moines! The brothers stole a glance at each other. Des Moines was not too far from Ames and Ma!

"So you boys better read or think of something else to do," said the conductor.

"We'll do that," said Ed. He noted that Mr. S. W. Pierce, the Davenport Soldiers' Home director who had journeyed to Glenwood to supervise them, seemed very busy with record books at a seat in the back of the train car.

Ed and Billy plotted their escape under their breaths. When the Burlington reached the Des Moines train station, they would separate themselves from the others, then make a dash for their freedom!

*Maybe times are better at home, and Ma can make us some gingerbread,* thought Billy. He had dreamed of Ma's gingerbread many a night at Glenwood, only to wake up longing for the fragrant, moist treat.

But it was not to be.

Ed told his pal Davey Littleton of their plans, and Davey informed Mr. Pierce of the plot. Unbeknown to the boys, S. W. Pierce considered runaways his specialty. In the past, he had traveled all over Iowa to catch boys who escaped the demands of his well-organized, efficient orphanage. The quiet, bespectacled Mr. Pierce suddenly metamorphosed into a tall, frightening personage with a bottom-of-the-well deep voice.

"So, you boys want to run away," he confronted Ed and Billy.

They stared at him, too frightened to move.

"Seems like you need me to keep you company on this trip." Mr. Pierce sat down beside the Sunday brothers and remained with them every moment of the rest of the trip.

*I'm gonna get Davey Littleton*, thought Billy. *Just wait till I catch 'im alone!*

Billy would have to postpone his revenge for a time. He and Ed spent eight hours a day, every day for the next week, marching around a track in front of the administration building of the Davenport Soldiers' Home, where Mr. Pierce kept a cool, unrelenting eye on them. Billy was almost glad to do laundry and dishes when the runaway punishment ended.

Davenport was not that different from Glenwood, Billy decided. He found new friends, as well as those who had come from the other orphanage with them. He enjoyed an occasional fight and endured the inevitable punishment that accompanied it. He and Ed continued to struggle in school because of their lack of early education when they lived at home.

Billy tolerated his religious training only because Mrs. Pierce was in charge.

He looked up to Mr. Pierce because the director demanded respect and obedience, but Billy, along with all the other boys, adored the gentle woman who bandaged their hurts and brushed the hair from their eyes with a ready smile.

Billy enjoyed stories from the Old Testament about David and Joshua and other warlike heroes, but he detested being called a "little lamb," as some of his Sunday school teachers had done.

Mrs. Pierce knew better. "Do you boys know about God's armor?" she asked one Sunday afternoon as Billy wistfully watched the white clouds float freely in the bright blue sky outside the parlor window.

"Armor? You mean, like a knight with a sword?" Billy forgot to raise his hand.

"Yes, Billy, exactly like a knight." Mrs. Pierce began to read from Ephesians 6: " 'Finally, my brethren, be strong in the Lord, and in the power of his might. Put on the whole armour of God, that ye may be able to stand against the wiles of the devil.' "

Billy did not understand it all; the "thees" and "thous" of the King James English confused and bored him. But he liked the big sword that Mrs. Pierce showed the boys. She permitted each of the eleven-year-olds to hold the heavy weapon in its sheath, telling them, "This sword is strong and sharp like God's Word, the Bible. With it, you can defeat the devil."

Billy wanted to hold the weapon forever, but he had to let Gerald take his turn. *If I had a sword like that*, he thought, *that ol' devil couldn't run fast enough.*

"Ed, we're gonna go home! Ma says we can both come home!"

Billy waved his mother's letter as if it were a flag.

Ed smiled to see his brother so excited, and the two shoved each other joyously until the cows in the barn mooed restlessly. They returned to their task of feeding the animals.

"I just couldn't stay here without you, Ed!" Billy had held his breath, waiting for this letter. Ed, now sixteen, was required to leave the Davenport Soldiers' Home at the end of the school year. Billy, two years younger, would have had to remain if his mother had not consented to his returning home. "Ma says we can both come if we help with the chores at Grandpa's."

The elation faded a little from Ed's eyes. "I'm not so sure it will work out. Grandpa was awfully mad at us when we left."

"Oh, Ed, that was years ago. He won't remember." Billy grinned slyly. "You just don't want to leave Letty Hill."

Ed answered Billy with a punch on the arm, and the two tussled until they heard the dinner bell's welcome interruption.

"Ma! Ma!" Billy threw his arms around his mother's frail shoulders and held on as if he would never let go. Ed enclosed them both in an embrace, then turned to his half brother. "Leroy, you are a-growin' like a weed!"

" 'Most as tall as me," marveled Billy.

Their mother could not speak, she was so overcome. Four years. It had been four everlasting, endless years. She clung to them, tears rolling freely down her face.

"Looks like they've put some meat on you boys," said Squire Corey, who quietly stood in the background.

"Food was good," answered Ed. He picked up his satchel and looked his grandfather squarely in the eye.

"I showed 'em how you taught me to ride bareback!" said Billy eagerly. "Once we had a circus, and I won first prize for the best act!"

Jennie laughed and hugged him again. "You're going to tell me all about it while we eat dinner. I made chicken and dumplings, and you'd better be hungry!"

"And gingerbread?" Billy's mouth watered.

"Of course I made gingerbread. And two kinds of pie!"

The reunited family laughed and joked as they climbed into Squire Corey's wagon and headed for his house.

"I'm tellin' you, Ed, if he swears at me one more time or hits Leroy, I'm gonna knock him flat." Billy's eyes glittered.

"I know, Billy. Every day when he tells me how lazy I am, I want to pound him. But it would break Ma's heart." Not long after the brothers had arrived in Ames, Ed had fought with his grandfather and moved to a neighbor's. He still came back to help from time to time, mostly so he could visit his mother and siblings.

Billy sighed. How could he love and hate someone so much? During their first months back home, their grandfather had seemed grateful for their help on his farm. Although the squire would never have admitted it, his old bones ached early every morning when he had to do all the milking and feeding and plowing himself.

But now nothing pleased him. It was more than a fourteen-year-old could bear.

"I wish he wouldn't mention Albert when Ma's around," said Billy.

Squire Corey did not seem to understand this reminder hurt his daughter so badly that she could hardly drag through the day. When Albert had grown too big to handle, Jennie had been forced to send her mentally handicapped son to an institution. She had never stopped grieving for him.

"Don't expect him to be any better today," cautioned Ed.

Billy shrugged. "He said Leroy and I could go to town with him tomorrow. Hope he remembers."

Ed nodded and mopped the sweat from his forehead. "Giddyap, Sam!" He shook the lines over the old white plow horse's back. Billy took a heavy wooden bucket to a neighboring field, where he picked up rocks. Both rejoiced that Grandpa did not check on them that afternoon.

*Maybe his joints hurt so bad today, he don't want to come out to the field*, thought Billy.

Billy's mother did not have to awaken him early the next morning. He and Leroy were up and ready to go to town, their carefully hoarded money knotted in handkerchiefs deep in their pockets. The two wolfed down their buckwheat cakes and maple syrup, then made their way out to the barn.

"Good-bye! Have a good time!" Jennie called to her sons.

Billy waved back. "Maybe I can find something pretty for Ma in town," he whispered to Leroy.

"I really do think Billy's Pa's favorite," Jennie told the kitchen stove as she dished up breakfast for herself. "If only they would get along better! Trouble is, they're just too much alike."

Squire Corey was already muttering angrily about their supposed tardiness. When Billy and Leroy tried to hitch up the horses, they accidentally pulled the rings out of the yoke.

"Can't you do nothin' right?" the squire exploded. He poisoned the air with oaths.

For Billy, who had grown accustomed to Mr. Pierce's firm but considerate treatment, it was the last straw. He threw the harness down and stalked back to the house.

43

"What's wrong, Billy? What happened?" His mother had seen it all.

"Grandpa did it again." Ed, who had come over to visit his mother while the squire was out of the house, slammed down his coffee and followed Billy to the boys' bedroom upstairs.

Billy yanked his old satchel out and began to fill it with his meager belongings.

"Don't take long to pack when you don't have much." He smiled grimly at Ed.

"Where you goin', Billy? Where *can* you go?"

"Don't know. Maybe today I'll stay at Ma's empty old house, talk around town, find out where I can get a ride out of here. Maybe Nevada or Boone. Maybe even Des Moines."

"You ain't gonna get a ride all the way to Des Moines."

"Probably not." Billy's blue eyes clouded over.

"Stay here, Billy, just a little bit longer. Maybe the Morrisons will need another hand next fall."

"The Morrisons can hardly pay you, let alone me. I don't want to leave Ma or you and Leroy, but I just gotta, Ed. I can't take Grandpa one day more."

Ed stared at his feet, blinking to keep the tears back. Billy hugged him roughly, then headed downstairs. Jennie handed him a bag that smelled faintly of gingerbread. She kissed him lightly, as if afraid her face would smash into a thousand pieces if she moved her lips too much.

"Hurry, before Grandpa knows you're going," she said calmly.

Billy slipped out the side door without another word.

"What do you want, boy?"

Billy stared into the probing eyes in the sullen face. "I want a job," he said.

The man grunted. "A lot of people do." The eyes raked over Billy as if he were a field to be plowed. Billy had ridden a borrowed horse ten miles to Nevada, Iowa, but he was not as dusty as the foyer in the shabby little hotel. *You could sure use some help*, thought the teenager.

"You know how to work?"

"I was raised in a Soldiers' Home," Billy said. "I know how to cook, clean, do laundry, chop wood, read, and cipher."

"I ain't got nothin' to pay a two-bit kid."

Billy felt his face redden like the sunset at the prairie edge. "I'll work for room and board."

The man's face brightened a little. "The law ain't after you or nothin'?"

Billy gazed unblinkingly into the other's eyes. "No."

"All right," said the man, a little louder than necessary. "You'll call me Mr. Jackson, and you'll be up at four thirty every morning to build the fires, then you'll do whatever me or Tildy—that's Mrs. Jackson—tells you. Understand?"

"I understand."

"Well, take this here broom and sweep up a bit."

Billy was almost glad to get to work. *Guess I'm used to the Soldiers' Home and Ma's house*, he thought. *Mr. Pierce never would let the dust gather, and Ma always said we might be poor, but we didn't have to be dirty. I guess Mr. Jackson doesn't know that.*

Billy rarely had time for homesickness. He chopped and hauled wood, did kitchen chores, made beds, helped Mrs. Jackson with the cooking, and often spent the night at the front desk in case any night travelers came in on the train. At times Mr. Jackson fretted about how the fire was built or when the mattresses were last turned, but most of the time he was content to let his wife and Billy take care of the hotel while he played cards with his friends in the saloon across the street. Occasionally he got roaring drunk, but Billy, remembering his stepfather's binges, knew enough to make himself scarce until Jackson recovered. While Billy sometimes grew tired of the endless work, he enjoyed his freedom from his grandfather's everlasting criticism.

After several months, however, he began to miss his home. *Wonder if Leroy's grown bigger than me by now. Maybe Ed's got his hound dog.* Ed had scrimped for months so he could buy one of the Morrisons' puppies when their bluetick delivered. *Wonder if Grandpa's forgiven me for leaving. . . .* Billy would turn his attention back to the kettle he was scrubbing for a while. But soon his thoughts would meander back to his home. Home. Ma. *Ma.* Tears would well up like a flood, and he would duck his head over his work so the Jacksons did not see.

"Mr. Jackson, I want to go home."

The man's head snapped back as if he had been napping. "Home? You quittin', boy?"

"No, no, Mr. Jackson, I just want to go see my ma in Ames for a day."

"Let the boy go, Cy." Mrs. Jackson surprised Billy almost as much as her husband. Tildy Jackson, a faded, bony woman, rarely spoke her mind.

"But we're almost full, Tildy. It ain't a good time—"

"No time is a good time, I reckon. But Billy here, he works hard. He needs to see his ma, and she needs to see him." The woman nailed her husband to the wall with her stare.

"All right, but be back day after tomorrow." Jackson stalked out the door and across the street to the saloon.

"I—I don't want to leave you to do all the work," stuttered Billy.

"It'll only be for a day or so." Tildy Jackson's face lit up with the first genuine smile Billy had seen. She pushed him gently. "Now you skedaddle upstairs and finish up. You'll want to leave real early tomorrow so you can see your ma!"

Faster. Faster. The raw, chilly wind yanked at his coat and reddened his face, but Billy ignored it, increasing his speed as he approached his grandfather's farm, pulled as if by a magnet.

Billy saw the barn first, weathered and formidable as his grandfather. Then he spotted the clothesline, full of frozen shirts dancing in the cold like stiff, wooden puppets. His mother was heaping them in her basket.

"Ma! Ma! I've come home!"

Clothespins fell from Jennie's mouth, and she ran faster than Billy thought she could. Jennie, laughing and crying, threw her arms around her son. "Billy! Are you home for good?"

Billy hugged her. "No, Ma. I've got a job in Nevada, and I'm just here for a visit."

"A long one?" asked a deep voice behind them.

Billy and Jennie turned to see Squire Corey standing by the barn door.

Billy took a deep breath. "No, Grandpa. I have to be back tomorrow."

"He's here for a *short* visit," said Jennie. She put her arms around Billy defiantly.

Squire Corey looked at them for a long minute.

"Maybe he can tell us the news over Nevada-way," he said and went back into the barn.

Jennie clasped her son ecstatically. "He really has missed you, even though he'll never say so. Help him feed the stock, and I'll cook you a dinner that'll make up for your birthday *and* Christmas!"

"I don't think you ought to walk back to Nevada in this kind of weather," said Jennie.

Billy scanned the sullen, chilly dawn and the purple-gray clouds off to the west. He hated even to think about fighting the wind for ten miles. The kitchen glowed in the kerosene lamplight as if it had absorbed his mother's joy. His warm, bulging stomach reminded him of all the delicious food he had consumed since coming back to Ames.

"Ed might make it over this evening again if you stay," continued his mother.

"Maybe he'll bring Lucy again!" Leroy adored his brother's lively little bluetick puppy.

"Weather's pretty bad," observed Squire Corey, sipping his boiling-hot coffee from his saucer, as he always did.

Billy could hardly believe his ears. Did his grandfather actually want him to *stay*?

"Guess I better wait another day. Maybe it'll clear up by tomorrow morning." Billy removed his boots and wiggled his toes near the red-hot stove.

"I ain't leavin' the latch out for any no-good, lazy liar like you!"

Mr. Jackson slurred his words, but Billy could hear him clearly through the stout oak door. He could hear, too, as the man swore and railed at him at the top of his voice.

"Mr. Jackson, I just stayed another day because of the storm!" The snow swirled and eddied around Billy in the twilight. *Today wasn't any better, but I came anyway.* "Please let me in, Mr. Jackson!"

"Go back to your mamma, boy! You ain't workin' here no more!" Billy heard Jackson stumble, then fall to the floor. Silence.

Billy hammered desperately on the door as the wind blew harder and harder. *Can't walk back home, not in this wind. What will I do? Where will I go?* He sank down on the front step in despair.

A small rattle above his head caught his attention. Who was tapping on the window? Mrs. Jackson looked even more ghostlike than usual, outlined against the upstairs window. She pointed behind her, then took the lantern toward the hallway. Billy sneaked around the hotel to the back door. It opened to admit him to the heavenly warmth of the kitchen.

"Sit there by the fire and eat some beans," was all she said, but Billy thought her words were the best he had ever heard. He gobbled down the hot food. Mrs. Jackson threw a heavy quilt around his shoulders.

"I'll lock the kitchen door when I go out," she said. "Don't make any noise, and he'll likely sleep through breakfast time."

"Thanks, Mrs. Jackson," said Billy.

"I can't do nothin' about his firin' you, but I wouldn't even leave a dog out on an evening like this, hungry and cold. I wish you could stay, Billy."

He smiled wearily as she left him and clutched his quilt as he lay down on the floor.

*I bet you wish you could go*, he thought as he drifted off to sleep.

# FIVE

I s this Colonel Scott's house?"

"Yes." The maid in her starched white apron looked at Billy questioningly.

"I heard he needed a hand to work around the place." The words flattened against his throat.

"What is your name?"

"Billy Sunday, ma'am."

"Well, Billy Sunday, wait here, and I will see if the master wants to talk with you."

Billy minded the cold less because the sun was shining today. Still, he would have liked to have stepped inside and waited near a fire. It seemed like a half hour before the maid returned.

"Please come in. Colonel Scott will see you in the back parlor."

A thankful Billy scraped his feet and took his cap off. *Ma, I hope you're praying for me. If I don't get this job, it means no supper tonight.* Yet how could he hope to work for the former lieutenant governor of Iowa?

"Hello, Billy." The tall, distinguished-looking man regarded him with piercing hazel eyes.

"Good morning, sir."

"Have you taken care of animals? Horses?"

"Oh, yes, sir. I was raised on a farm, then helped out in the barn when I lived at the Soldiers' homes in Glenwood and Davenport."

"Father in the war?"

"Yes, sir." *Please, Colonel Scott, I need this job so much. Please.*

The colonel asked him more questions about his background and skills, then took him out to the stables, where he introduced Billy to his twenty Shetland ponies. When they returned to the house, he called to his wife, "Tessie, this young man wants to work for us. I think he may be what we're looking for."

The plump, pretty woman swept in, a vision of satin skirts and tinkling earrings. But she fixed shrewd blue eyes on Billy. "He's not very big," said Mrs. Scott. "Is he strong enough? Can he scrub and do heavy work?"

"I sure can, Mrs. Scott," declared Billy. "I worked hard at the orphanage, and I will work hard here."

"Then come clean the cellar stairs," said Mrs. Scott. "If you wash those dirty stairs well, then maybe you'll do." She called to the maid, who brought a scrub brush, bucket, and soap. "Let me know when he's finished."

Billy filled the bucket with water he heated on the stove, determined to make those cellar steps the cleanest ones this side of heaven.

"My, my!" said the surprised woman when Billy notified the maid of his completed task. "Those really *are* spotless."

"See, my dear. My character judgments are usually accurate," teased the colonel.

"Apparently they are. You may help Martha in the kitchen this evening," said Mrs. Scott.

"Tomorrow," said Colonel Scott, "I'll take you back to the stable, and we'll talk horseflesh."

"Thank you." The gratitude in Billy's throat crowded out any other words.

"It's too late for you to go to school this term," explained the colonel, "but we will plan to send you next fall."

*School?* Stifling memories of afternoons in the orphanage schoolroom squeezed Billy's brain, but he said nothing. He had a job; that was enough.

Billy enjoyed his work at the Scotts' home. They expected much of him, but they were fair and treated him with respect. Eight dollars a month plus room and board seemed lucrative after his hotel job.

Billy's new employers, the first wealthy people he had ever known, fascinated him. They discussed politics and literature, as well as local events, and did not hesitate to share their knowledge with him. Billy had never considered a life in which survival was not the key issue of each day.

The Scotts insisted that Billy attend Nevada High School, a public school far more advanced academically than most Iowa high schools.

Billy struggled, as always, because of his lack of early education, but the teachers and student body soon became aware of his oratorical gifts. "Speaking a piece" was an entertainment included in every program. When audiences heard that Billy was to recite "Horatius at the

Bridge" or "Spartacus and the Gladiators," classrooms and school auditoriums filled quickly. Nathaniel Parker Willis's "Parrhasius and the Captive," a dark, dramatic poem about a captive who was tortured and finally murdered in order that a Greek artist could study his face and movements as he painted the scene, overwhelmed stunned audiences.

But Billy never stayed serious for long. Teachers remembered him as a practical jokester who had a finger in every comedic pie in their classrooms.

His limited leisure time kept him out of trouble. Besides his work at Colonel Scott's, Billy also became the high school janitor, rising at 2:00 A.M. every day to build fourteen fires. He also had to maintain the fires throughout the day, as well as sweep and carry out other janitorial duties.

Employment demands could not, however, deplete Billy's amazing store of energy.

Above all other things, Billy could run.

And run.

And run!

One day a strong, wiry young man strode into town, boasting that he could beat anyone in a footrace, anytime, anywhere. The Nevada populace took exception to his bragging; everyone knew Billy Sunday could run faster than anyone in town! The loafers at Stanton's general store called for a contest and cheered wildly when Billy left the braggart far behind.

Billy was fast, they all agreed afterward, slapping each other on the back and spitting tobacco juice farther than usual. But the real test was the Ames Fourth of July 100-yard dash. How would their young speedster do then?

The Fourth arrived, a perfect, cloudless day seemingly

designed for picnics, homemade ice cream, and five-cents-a-glass lemonade stored in an underground vat to keep it cold. Hundreds of patriotic citizens applauded speeches and shook hands with local politicians, reveling in the background of marching-band music and red, white, and blue bunting. Cannons from nearby Iowa State College thundered in a salute to the holiday.

Then the real drama finally began. Fourteen lined up for the 100-yard dash, including the projected winner, a professor from the college, sportily attired in a rose-colored running suit and special shoes. Billy rolled up his overalls and took off his shirt. He wiggled his toes in the hot Iowa summertime dust. Billy could hardly wait to hear the starting gun.

"On your mark—get set—GO!"

The crowd whooped and hollered as the men surged ahead. Halfway through the race, three favorites emerged: the professor, a farmer named Bates, and Billy, the only teenager. Bates fell behind the others at seventy-five yards, and Billy owned the finish line, with the professor trailing five yards behind him.

"Hurrah for Billy Sunday! Hurrah!"

Colonel Scott said, "I knew the boy had it in him!" and accepted congratulations all around.

Billy's family had come to Ames to watch the race. His mother forgot her usual reserve in town and screamed ecstatically, waving her handkerchief. Squire Corey said, "That 'un always could outrun a deer." Leroy danced around Billy. "Three whole dollars! Whatcha gonna do with the prize, Billy?"

Billy could not answer right away, as his brother Ed, his classmates, and other supporters lifted him to their shoulders and carried him away in triumph.

But later Billy bought his mother and grandfather large glasses of lemonade. His brothers ate the biggest ice cream cones they had ever seen, as Billy spent all his prize money to treat his friends.

"Colonel, I don't want to go through with the graduation program."

"Not attend the graduation ceremonies? But why, Billy? You've worked so hard to get through high school. We're all proud of you. They'll certainly want you to make a speech."

"I know, Colonel Scott, and I appreciate you and Mrs. Scott very much. I'd 'a never made it if you hadn't believed I could do it." Billy squirmed a little, but he had made up his mind. "I want to move to Marshalltown."

"Marshalltown?"

"The fire brigade there—they want me to join them." Billy gave Colonel Scott the letter that had arrived the day before. The Marshalltown, Iowa, brigade boasted a fine reputation among the many companies in the state. The teams competed in running, ladder climbing, and hose-cart racing. Hose-cart racing was a dangerous contest in which groups of twelve men hauled quarter-ton two-wheeled carts carrying rolls of fire hoses to hydrants three hundred yards distant. If an Iowa town was fortunate enough to sponsor a winning fire brigade, its status rose immediately.

Colonel Scott slowly read, then folded the letter. "Well, I can see why you want to do it."

"I'll say! I don't want them to find somebody else before I can get there!"

Colonel Scott shook Billy's hand, then placed his hands on the eager teen's shoulders. "Billy, you've been a hard worker and a good boy. We will miss you, but we know there are great things in store for you."

Billy tried to keep his face still, but he felt his lower lip quiver. "Thank you, Colonel. I will never forget you."

"Do it this way," said the furniture store owner, deftly spreading the varnish on the new chair.

Billy tried to hold his brush the way Mr. Wilbur did, but somehow the stain always ran in globby streams down the chair legs. At eighteen, he enjoyed his independence, but how he hated his new job in Marshalltown! Mr. Wilbur and Mr. Upson also ran an undertaker's service, and Billy found himself driving caskets to the cemetery, standing by open graves as mourners wept. *If it weren't for the fellows on the fire brigade and the baseball team, I'd go back to Colonel Scott's in a second.*

But the brigade had welcomed Billy with open arms. His speed, they said, would make a major impact in the state competition, in which fifteen thousand men participated.

Charlie Stroud, a fellow sprinter, also invited Billy to the Marshalltown baseball game with Newton. "Take a look at us, Billy," he urged. "We sure could use you in the outfield."

Baseball, a relatively new game in 1880, had taken the country by storm. Every town of any size had an amateur team and strove to attract the best players whether rich, poor, immigrant, or natural-born citizen. The passion for the sport broke down walls in communities as supporters of "our boys" yelled encouragement to people they would not have spoken to on the streets. Baseball represented a town's prosperity and vitality, an opportunity to express area pride.

Billy went to the game and watched the Marshall-town team struggle with the Newton batters. He always had played catch, but he had little experience playing the organized game. The rules differed from place to place, and he found it all confusing.

"Come to our practice," Charlie begged. "You're a natural. I just know it."

Billy did, and Marshalltown had one more reason to cheer for the blond sprinter. Billy made an immediate difference in their won/lost record. His blinding speed and innate coordination often inspired the home crowd to stand whenever a ball was batted his way. They did not want to miss a single catch Billy made.

When the Marshalltown team played Des Moines in the state finals in 1882, Billy put on a fielding show with his now-famous speed, taking dives into the grass and leaping high into the air to capture the ball. He also scored five runs, and Marshalltown won its first state title since 1867, when Adrian "Cap" Anson, a member of the Chicago White Stockings, fielded for its team. Cap had gone on to become one of America's top players.

Anson's aunt Em still took honors as Marshalltown's most rabid fan. She wrote her nephew constantly about the young outfielder who did the impossible. When Cap came home to visit, she told a hundred stories about her favorite Marshalltown ballplayer.

"Cap," insisted Aunt Em, "you have to see this boy run and catch. No one can match him."

Anson grinned easily at the persistent old lady. "Well, if you say so, I know he must be the best player in the whole world."

"Not the best," said his father, Henry, "but a good one."

Cap looked at him. "That good?"

"That good."

Aunt Em talked on and on. As Cap nodded pleasantly at her, he privately categorized his team's needs and weighed the possibilities. *Maybe. Maybe this boy would be worth a try.*

"Mr. Wilbur, I'm sorry to leave so sudden, but I'm goin' to Chicago tomorrow."

The furniture store owner looked up from the chair he was staining to see his assistant's apologetic but shining face. Billy handed his boss a telegram.

"So you're going to play baseball for the Chicago White Stockings," said the taciturn man.

"Sure hope to. They want me to try out for the team."

Mr. Wilbur's face split into the widest smile Billy had ever seen. "Well, you never will be any good at makin' furniture," he said, shaking Billy's hand heartily, "but I'd bet my last dollar that you're one of the best ballplayers around. You'll make us all proud!"

*Maybe I'm crazy. Maybe nothin' will come of it, nothin' at all.* Billy hardly dared to breathe as he rode the train. He didn't want to break the spell that the telegram had cast on him.

*Ma was happy, but she was worried about my leaving a steady job. Ed said Chicago was a bad place—no place for an Iowa farm boy to live. But everybody thinks I can play on the White Stockings team. Everybody.*

Billy fingered the dollar in the pocket of his green six-dollar suit and clutched the handle of his valise tightly. In a few more hours, he'd arrive in Chicago.

*Can I do it? I'll soon know.*

# SIX

"Billy, I want you to race Fred Pfeffer, our second baseman." Cap Anson, the hard-hitting first baseman and outfielder, was not only the team leader; he also functioned as manager of the White Stockings. The team president, A. G. Spalding, depended on Anson's judgment in finding new talent.

To the other White Stockings' amusement, Billy removed his shoes and waited for instructions. Mike "King" Kelly, the team's legendary catcher, and Ned Williamson, a powerful hitter, exchanged glances.

*Probably can't even grow a mustache*, thought Kelly, scrutinizing the blond youngster. At twenty, Billy stood five feet ten inches and weighed 160 pounds. *Not near big enough to hit a ball. What can Cap be thinking of? Pfeffer will finish off this hayseed real quick.* The King knew that the second baseman ran the bases faster than anyone else on the team.

Anson set the boundaries of the 100-yard dash.

Billy and Pfeffer lined up.

"Ready."

"Set."

"GO!"

Billy shot in front of the astonished Pfeffer almost immediately, finishing the race well ahead of him. The rest of the White Stockings stood motionless, too amazed to cheer.

Cap Anson chuckled. "Told you boys we grow 'em good in Marshalltown!"

King Kelly sauntered over to the boy, who was brushing off his pants, and stuck out his big hand. "Glad you came to see us, lad," he said as the other players followed suit. "Welcome to the Chicago White Stockings."

Baseball had flourished in the United States since the 1860s. Most towns of any size boasted a local amateur team, and larger cities supported professional players. Because of the telegraph, newspapers and magazines could receive scores quickly, and editors began to take notice of the sport. Journalists often traveled with the teams, sending information back home for eager fans to peruse in newly planned sports sections.

The game rules were still largely undefined, as each year league rules committees welcomed suggestions from game participants, audiences, umpires, managers, and owners. In the 1880s, a batter was permitted three strikes. He could, however, tell the umpire where he wished the ball to be thrown, high or low. The umpire would then inform the pitcher. If the batter did not swing at a pitch thrown where he had asked, the umpire called a strike. If balls were pitched in unsolicited areas, they were considered "unfair"; seven unfair balls sent the batter to first base. Pitchers could not throw overhand in the National League until 1884. For several years, National League rules dictated that batters could use a bat with one flat side. Early baseball players did not use much equipment. Catchers were the first to wear padded gloves and masks as they took their vulnerable position behind home plate. But only a few other defensive players wore half-fingered gloves; most fielders considered them effeminate.

The baseball teams trained and paid the game umpires until a movement in the 1880s shifted that responsibility to the leagues in an effort to increase the umpires' impartiality.

Techniques now accepted as standard, such as the "backing up" of fielders, sacrifice hitting, bunting, and stealing bases, all developed and became an integral part of the game during the 1880s.

During this exciting formative period, young Billy Sunday arrived in Chicago to join one of the most dominant teams in baseball history. The White Stockings had already won the National League pennant in 1880, 1881, and 1882.[1] They would triumph twice more during the decade, as well as taking runner-up honors twice and placing third twice.[2] Lake Front Park, where the team played, seated ten thousand fans, who comprised the biggest home audience in baseball. The stadium included a band shell by the main gate and eighteen luxurious private boxes. President Spalding communicated with Anson down in the clubhouse with the newly installed telephone in his box. Both Spalding and Anson wanted to project a proper image, so team members always enjoyed road trips on splendid Pullman trains. They stayed in excellent hotels, arriving in ballparks in deluxe carriages drawn by gorgeous horses. Players were required to appear in evening dress for dinner. "First-class" described every-thing connected with the White Stockings.

"What kind of socks are these, anyway?" Billy asked as the players readied for their first game of the season.

"Those are silk," answered Pfeffer, grinning. After the initial race between the two, he and Billy had be-come good friends. "You'll soon get used to 'em, Billy."

Billy shook his head. He sometimes felt as if he had landed on the moon. He loved Chicago, but the enor-mous buildings, the crowded streets, the bewildering mix of Italian, Irish, Polish, Slavic, and black populations made his head swim. He had not slept well the night be-fore because he was accustomed to quiet rural nights, not the street noises that continued outside his hotel room into the wee hours of the morning.

*But that's not why you couldn't sleep*, he admitted to himself. *You knew that this is* the *day.*

His toes twitched in the new socks, as if they could not wait to run the bases.

But it was not to be. On May 22, 1883, Billy braved the thirty-two-degree wind off Lake Michigan and the clever Boston Beaneater pitcher "Grasshopper" Jim Whit-ney, only to strike out all four times he came to bat.

Cap Anson slapped the shoulder of the dejected young outfielder.

"Don't worry, Billy. It'll come. You and I just have some work to do."

Cap, an eventual Hall of Famer who batted .300 and above almost all of his twenty-two years of baseball,[3] patiently tutored his young protégé. After a humiliat-ing series of eleven strikeouts, Billy finally connected with the ball on July 25 in Chicago, when the White Stockings defeated Philadelphia 11–2. He hit twice out

of five times at bat and caught two balls in the outfield.[4]
The press and the spectators began to take note of Billy's
speed. He only hit the ball once out of four times at bat
during his August 2 game against New York (it rolled just
twenty-five feet past first base), but Billy's swift feet made
him safe before the fielder could return to his base.[5]

Billy also began to steal bases. Chicago fans rejoiced
to see him hit a single; they knew it was a prelude to a
daredevil contest with the pitcher.

*See me here on first base, pitcher? See me here on second?
You ain't goin' to see me here long!*

Anson had to warn Billy about his fearlessness.
Sometimes, he counseled, a player should *stay* on base! He
also had to take Billy to task because he occasionally forgot to tag a base in his haste to reach the next one. Even
Cap, whom Billy loved and respected, did not always
make an impression on the hungry young base stealer. At
the least provocation, Billy was off and running.

Chicago audiences loved it. They endured his mediocre hitting as long as they could watch him run the bases.
"If only he could steal first base!" joked his supporters.[6]

Billy committed many errors in the outfield, but
some of his catches were so brilliant, they remained in
the minds of observers long after the game. He played
right field most of the time, substituting for Anson
when he was needed elsewhere.

As Billy became known throughout the Chicago area,
Goodwin and Company included his picture on baseball
cards tucked in their packages of Old Judge and Gypsy
Queen cigarettes. D. Buchner and Company sold chew-
ing tobacco with baseball cards that also included a
smooth-faced portrait of Billy.

Cap Anson, too, made plans to publicize his newest

player. Why not organize races where Billy could show off his blinding speed? He planned a 100-yard dash after a game in Buffalo on August 11, matching Billy against a professional runner named Kittleman for a prize of fifty dollars. Billy tried to talk his manager out of the race but could not change his mind. He lost, but Anson's faith in his abilities remained immovable.

Cap convinced Spalding to retain Billy for the 1884 season, even though his initial year was less than spectacular. He had found Billy hardworking, positive, and eager to learn. Disciplined and orderly, Anson approved the rookie's lifestyle, so different from those of his teammates. Billy's temper sometimes got him into fights, but his strict orphanage upbringing had tempered the wild streak in him. He readily accepted responsibilities that were often dumped on substitute players with little status: taking tickets at the gate, managing receipts, running travel arrangements. Convinced of his recruit's integrity, Anson gave Billy far broader duties than most managers assigned to players. At times he entrusted Billy with a suitcase containing thousands of dollars as the team traveled. For Billy, Cap helped fill the emptiness left when his father had died.

Such favoritism should have caused tension within the team; but the other players liked and respected Billy. They knew he would give his all in whatever he did. A few critics demanded Anson find another substitute outfielder with more firepower, but most of the Chicago fans enjoyed his running so much, they were willing to believe his batting average would improve.

During the off-season, Billy went home to Marshalltown to work at whatever job he could find. He had made about $720 as a rookie, which was considered a good living (most factory workers earned $500 a year). But Billy hated sitting around; he figured he would work until early spring, when Anson gathered his ballplayers for preseason training, a novel concept at that time.

Anson began the 1884 season with a stern warning to his team about drinking and curfews. King Kelly smiled easily and agreed readily. Anson knew better than to trust his affability; the King charmed everyone, then did what he wanted. He drank heavily, yet seemed unaffected by the alcohol when he played. He dazzled Chicago during baseball season with his powerful bat and his "Kelly spread," a special technique he developed to avoid being tagged out. Earnest Thayer, the author of "Casey at the Bat," pointed to King Kelly as his inspiration; and saloon pianists throughout Chicago played one of the most popular songs of the day, "Slide, Kelly, Slide." Chicago fans soon sang it every time he got on base. During off-season, the King shone as a vaudeville performer. Handsome and charismatic, he rarely appeared in public without a lovely girl on either arm.

Anson surveyed the rest of his players, congratulating himself on their brilliance. Besides King Kelly, he had put together Chicago's "Stone Wall," an infield that rarely let a ball past them: Fred Pfeffer at second base, Tom Burns at shortstop, Ned Williamson at third base, and himself at first. Abner Dalrymple and George Gore regularly patrolled the outfield with Kelly, and Frank "Silver" Flint, an intelligent, steady catcher, worked with superb pitchers Larry Corcoran and Fred Goldsmith. Anson sighed; if only his players handled their lives as well as they handled fly balls! Most of them tried to outdo King Kelly in wild, uninhibited living. Anson was no moralist, but he knew such debauchery would affect their games.

Anson glanced at Billy, who was distributing equipment. If only all his players lived like Billy Sunday! The young man enjoyed spending time with his teammates, but he drank only moderately and often ordered lemonade or sarsaparilla when his friends guzzled shot after shot of whiskey. He went to bed early and always reported on time for team meetings. The fans loved him. Even ladies who disliked baseball did not mind attending the games when the clean-cut, polite young man from Iowa doffed his cap to them before the game.

Anson grinned wryly. He was glad the rest of the team did not bat like Billy Sunday! But, with a little tutoring, the boy might have a better season in 1884.

Anson arranged for another 100-yard-dash race between Billy and Fred Pfeffer. This time, however, he scheduled the contest right before an exhibition game in Chicago. Billy again won handily, and this public display of his speed calmed rumors that Anson kept him on the payroll as his personal flunky.

Billy did exhibit more promise in the spring of 1884. Anson had to take catcher Flint's place because of an injury, so Billy played sixteen games straight, crossing home plate nine times for the White Stockings. His fielding, however, ruined the positive trend: He committed eight errors in twenty-five fielding opportunities. Two of those mistakes occurred at critical points, costing Chicago victories.[7]

The rest of the team played poorly during the initial part of the 1884 season, posting a record of only four victories out of sixteen games.[8] A. G. Spalding, the White Stockings' president, sent an indignant message to his team at the end of May: Deliver, or else! He deplored the players' uncontrolled drinking and undisciplined ways. Spalding told Anson he had his permission to hire private detectives to make sure the players made their 11:00 P.M. bedtime curfew.

Such tactics had little positive effect. Chicago finished fourth at the end of the 1884 season, their most disappointing showing in the 1880s. Billy's batting average (.222) hovered near that of a typical National League player, but his fielding deteriorated as the season went on.[9] By the end of 1884, he ranked dead last in the National League. But Anson continued to support Billy as the only team member who kept the rules and worked consistently on his game, so he was included as a reserve in the 1885 season roster.

A. G. Spalding replaced pitchers Goldman, who suffered a chronic injury, and the unstable, sickly Corcoran with future Hall of Famer John Clarkson and Jim McCormick, a reliable pitcher who had anchored various other teams.

Spalding also instigated a monetary reward/punishment system. If team members were discovered drinking, they paid stringent fines. If they complied with the complete abstinence rule during training, they were to receive equivalent bonuses.

The approach seemed to motivate the White Stockings. They won constantly during May and June of 1885.

Billy did not see much action, but he played well when he did, hitting in thirteen of thirty-six at bats, posting a team best during those months.[10] When he slammed a ball among the buggies and carriages parked outside the stadium, the Chicago crowd erupted with a roar. Some players might jog slowly around the bases after such a home run, but not Billy! He gave it his all, as usual, and the fans yelled in approval as he crossed home plate. He committed no errors in his fielding during that time. His reputation as a base stealer grew.

Billy was learning to strategize his batting; he no longer tried to smash the ball out of the stadium every time. If he just made contact with the ball, chances were good that he could make it to first base. His batting improved, as did his confidence. In August 1885 Billy made two spectacular catches of fly balls before an ecstatic home crowd and knocked two triples and a home run to help his team to more victories.[11]

Cap Anson had not given up his idea to race Billy against the best. He planned a 100-yard dash before one of the August games, in which Billy was to compete with a runner named Leon Loser. No loser he, the sprinter had defeated a bicycle rider in a race not long before.

"Sunday's fast, but he can't beat a man like that," said a cynical observer.

"He'll beat him! He's the best base runner in the whole wide world!" retorted a little boy sitting near him.

Billy bounced and stretched, readying himself for the race. "On your mark, get set, GO!" The two runners dashed for the finish line, but the shorter, blonder blur won out. Billy had defeated the favorite!

It seemed as if all Chicago took the victory personally.

Billy's triumph certainly pleased A. G. Spalding. It fit into his ultimate goal: to make baseball a respectable family entertainment for the upper and middle classes. The American League, his competition, promoted games on Sunday with twenty-five-cent admission prices and availability of alcohol in the ballparks. Such a setup catered to factory employees, whose only day off was Sunday. Most were immigrants who considered a glass of beer essential to a relaxing day off. Spalding believed he would increase his profits in the long run if he targeted the upper classes. Despite neighborhood protests, he moved his team to the opulent thirty-thousand-dollar West Side Ball Park off Congress Avenue in the most populous section of Chicago. Convenient transportation by train or trolley brought families to watch the White Stockings for a fifty-cent admission. In compliance with local conservatism, Spalding scheduled no games on Sunday and prohibited the consumption of alcohol in his park. He hoped the reputable surroundings would have a positive influence on his ballplayers.

Billy finished the 1885 season with his usual combination of brilliant and botched plays. His dramatic catches and excellent base running contrasted with his increase in errors and decrease in batting average. But he never bored the Chicago fans. No one ever knew just what Billy Sunday would do when he headed for the out-field or ran the bases.

When catcher Flint again injured his hand, Anson inserted Billy in the lineup for an important series between the top-ranked White Stockings and second-place New York. Billy outdid himself, turning a single into a triple by his dazzling baserunning. He made a difficult catch despite smashing into the right-field wall in the second game. In the fourth game, Billy walked to first base, sneaked to second, and then zipped home when New York made an error.[12]

The White Stockings achieved their first goal of the 1885 season: making the World Series! Spalding suspended George Gore, the team's center fielder, at the end of the regular playing season for poor play and frequent violation of the team abstinence rules. Cap Anson inserted Billy Sunday for the all-important series with the St. Louis Browns.

*I can't believe it*, thought Billy as he ran to the outfield. *Me, Billy Sunday, playing in a World Series. I must be back at the Soldiers' Home, asleep next to Ed.* But the sun polished the St. Louis stadium with its warm light, and the crisp autumn air reassured him he was not dreaming. *Better keep alert, boy*, Billy told himself. *You got important things to do today.*

Billy stood at the plate, as he had hundreds of times. *Wish I was back in Marshalltown, when the pitching wasn't so tough to hit.* He had not batted well in the first game of the series. But now he calmed his rebellious stomach, gripped the bat, and faced the St. Louis pitcher. *Cr-r-r-ack!* Billy attacked first base, then sped to second before the outfield could recover. While the home crowd *ohh-h*ed in dismay, the few Chicago fans rioted in the stands. Cap Anson grinned from ear to ear and waved his cap at Billy. Relief washed over Billy like a postgame shower. A double!

Billy smiled innocently at the pitcher, who scowled. The young runner stuck a toe as far to the right as he could without leaving base. The pitcher forced himself to focus on the next batter as Billy casually slipped off the bag.

*Third base. Third base.* Billy hungered for it as if it were his mother's gingerbread. But when the pitcher whipped a couple of throws back to second base, Billy stood there as if he had never thought of moving. Unnerved, the pitcher threw wildly above the catcher. In a moment Billy blurred to third base, amid the cheers of the small but joyous Chicago crowd.

*Home. I'm going home.* Nothing would stop him. Nothing.

King Kelly tapped a weak grounder next, and Billy took off as if all the St. Louis fans were on his trail. He headed unswervingly for home plate as the umpire, stupefied by his swiftness, watched. Billy's speed so distracted him that he forgot to monitor first base, where the baseman deftly caught the pitcher's throw well before the King could reach base.

But the umpire called Kelly safe.

The St. Louis stadium nearly shifted from its foundation as thousands of fans roared with rage. Billy headed for the dugout as the crowd's anger seemed to grow and grow. *Even King Kelly better know he can't show off on this one,* Billy thought. For the first time, he feared for the White Stockings' safety.

Bewildered, then enraged, the mortified umpire declared the game a forfeit to Chicago, with a mythical score of Chicago 9, St. Louis 0 (actual score: Chicago 5, St. Louis 4). The roars turned to howls as Cap Anson hurried his players to their carriage and back to the hotel. Even the police assigned to escort them did not look overly friendly.

"Boys, we better mind our p's and q's," advised Anson at their early dinner. The players nodded. For once, they had no desire to sample the nightlife of St. Louis.

Billy played well for the remainder of the series, connecting with the ball six times in all and scoring five runs.[13] He made no errors in the outfield. At one point, however, he argued with the umpire so vehemently the man pronounced Billy a liar and threatened to close his mouth for him. Billy said no more, but his knuckles whitened. How they ached to flatten the man! Anson cajoled the enraged fielder back to the bench and mopped his own brow with his handkerchief.

*It's a tough one when my most upstanding player is almost thrown out for fighting with the umpire.* Hostility sat in the stands during the Chicago/St. Louis series of 1885. It pushed the umpires, managers, and players toward each other.

The end of the series brought no relief. St. Louis had in reality defeated Chicago 3–2, with another game tied, but the forfeited game given to Chicago produced an official tie (3–3–1) that rankled the minds of everyone.[14] Both teams filed protests.

The unscratched itch tingled anew when fans in both cities heard that Arlie Latham, the St. Louis Browns' legendary base runner, was to run a 100-yard dash with the White Stockings' Billy Sunday in November. The winner would receive five hundred dollars. Baseball supporters, players, and managers all bet exorbitantly on the contest, which was to be held in St. Louis. Some newspapers estimated that Sunday supporters put seventy-five thousand dollars on the line in Chicago. St. Louis fans also bet heavily on their favorite.

*Glad this race is in St. Louis,* thought Billy as he and Arlie stretched and warmed up in the mild fall air. *Sure would have been chilly in Chicago.*

He tightened the bows on his shoes.

*I'm gonna win. I know I'm gonna win.* Billy grinned determinedly.

"Ready." The thousand spectators drew in their breath together.

"Set." Pause. *Gotta win this one for Cap and the boys.*

"GO!"

Latham took the early lead, but Billy kept his eyes on the finish line. He pushed ahead near the end and defeated the St. Louis runner by three yards, running the race in 10.25 seconds![15]

Anson clapped Billy on the back; his fellow players mobbed him.

"Boys, you're gonna hurt my runner so he can't play next season!" Anson's plea went unheeded as Billy rode their shoulders in triumph. All Chicago toasted their favorite throughout the day as Billy and his friends celebrated in St. Louis. By nighttime, Billy, exhausted by the race and the festivities, wanted to go to bed early.

"Aw, Billy," protested his teammates, "don't you want to paint the town for once? It's off-season."

Billy grinned. "Reckon I'll take a turn with you boys when we get back to Chicago tomorrow night. But we're in St. Louis, in case you hadn't remembered. Might not be the best place to 'paint the town' at night."

Fred Pfeffer laughed and raised his glass anew. "To Billy Sunday, the smartest White Stocking, as well as the fastest!" The rest of the group followed suit, and Billy headed happily, but wearily, up to his room.

*We may not have won the World Series, but I'm glad I could win the race for my friends.*

# SEVEN

For the first time, Billy's 1885 batting average of .256 approached those of the upper third of league ball-players. Despite his boundless enthusiasm in fielding, he continued to struggle with making errors; he placed thirty-second of thirty-five for the 1885 season.[1] But A. G. Spalding and Anson still decided to retain him for the 1886 season as a reserve player.

Billy worked as a fireman during the off-season in Belle Plaine, Iowa, where he met Clara Nelson, the attractive daughter of a railroad engineer. Clara, who had an irrepressible sense of fun, helped make his winter a pleasant one.

Baptist evangelist Sam Jones had held meetings in Chicago from February through April, and thousands had attended, including the White Stockings' president Spalding. Jones had converted Spalding to Christianity and convinced him more than ever of the evils of alcohol. Although Spalding did *not* adopt Jones's dislike for baseball as a monumental waste of time and an evil influence on society, he firmly resolved that his players would take an abstinence pledge for the 1886 season.

At Cap Anson's insistence, he sent the team south for preseason training and therapy in Hot Springs, Arkansas, then Nashville, Tennessee. There Billy stayed behind to assist their pitcher, Jim McCormick, who had injured his ankle, while the rest of the team returned to Chicago.

*This season's gonna be better than '85*, he vowed when he arrived at the West Side Park in Chicago. Billy began with a promising six hits in nineteen at bats during May. His two stolen bases contributed to the three runs he scored, but he continued to make glaring errors in the outfield.[2]

*The boys don't give me a hard time, and Cap is right when he has to bench me, but I wish I could do better. Maybe he won't be able to convince Mr. Spalding to keep me in Chicago.* Billy's popularity continued with the fans and with his teammates, despite his struggles, but he found himself longing for his mother, Ed, and his friends back in Iowa.

Very late one warm June night as Billy and other baseball players were visiting nightspots and drinking their way across downtown Chicago, they heard, of all things, a hymn.

"Listen, boys! My mother used to sing that to me," said Billy. He followed the sound to a small band playing on the corner of State and Van Buren Streets.

"Come, on, Billy. We'll take you someplace where there's some *real* music," offered his companions.

"I want to stay." Billy sat down on the curb, and a number of the ballplayers sat down beside him to listen as the band played. A few mission workers sang hymn after hymn.

*I haven't heard songs like that since I left Davenport.* Billy could not take his eyes off the group. The music flowed over him like a warm river, soothing him. His uncertain future with the White Stockings floated away like leaves down the creek behind his grandfather's house.

*I want to stay right here. I'll stay all night, if only they'll sing another one. . . .*

"Come on down to the Pacific Garden Mission, fellows," urged Harry Monroe, one of the young musicians. "It's only a few blocks away. You'll find God there."

Billy stood. "I'm going." The others watched openmouthed as Billy followed Monroe down the street. The Pacific Garden Mission was located in one of the worst areas of Chicago, an area full of saloons, houses of prostitution, dirty dance halls, and gambling establishments. "Strangers Welcome" said the lantern-lit sign over the door.

*I do. I do feel at home here.*

He wondered why. The place reeked with tobacco and whiskey odors and the sweat and dirt of the men who sat on the rude wooden benches.

One emaciated man stood up, his face as fragile and yellowed as old paper. "I 'uz a drunk and a thief," he said, "but Jesus done come into my heart and made me as new and clean as a little newborn baby, and I know I'm goin' to heaven."

Most of the men stared at him and ducked their heads. An enormous black-haired man whose muscles bulged out of his shabby sleeves also rose. "I—I hurt a man bad once," he quavered. "Took his bottle of whiskey and smacked 'im with it, but the Lord done forgive me.

Now I can sleep without seein' his face and his blood afore me every night."

Billy sat motionless through the entire service as man after man told how Jesus had rescued him from misery and heartbreak. When Colonel Clark, the founder of the mission, invited the men to ask Jesus Christ into their hearts, Billy did not move. He watched one man finally lurch forward. The colonel and Harry put their arms around the filthy, half-drunken derelict and prayed.

Later, as he stared at the ceiling in his room, Billy could hear the hymn that had drawn him to the mission. "Amazing grace, how sweet the sound, that saved a wretch like me. . . ." He knew he was too far away from the Pacific Garden Mission to hear the actual music, but the words wafted as tantalizingly through his room as the fragrance of his mother's Christmas dinners.

Billy knew he would return to the place that welcomed strangers.


"Young man, do you want to know Jesus Christ as your best friend? Do you want to ask Him to forgive your sins?"

The woman's gentle, precise voice held Billy as if she had gripped his coat lapels. Her wise eyes penetrated his.

"Y—yes, ma'am, I believe I do." The well-dressed young man had returned a few nights after Mrs. Clark had first spotted him. The boy's clean-cut appearance contrasted so vividly with that of the pitiful creatures around him. *But God is never fooled by appearance*, Mrs. Clark reminded herself. *He needs Christ as much as any of us here at the mission.* Her eyes glanced at the large inscription on the wall: "Christ Came into the World to Save Sinners, Among Whom I Am Chief." Her husband, an astute Chicago businessman who had been involved in the Board of Trade, had recognized his own need for God's forgiveness and asked Jesus Christ to be his Savior. Moved by the suffering of the people he saw each day in downtown Chicago, he had poured his entire fortune into the mission, hoping to rescue as many as he could. Colonel Clark himself had nailed that large sign on the wall.

Now the quiet man approached his wife and Billy. "Billy wants to invite Christ into his life," said Mrs. Clark.

The colonel smiled, and Billy thought he would fall over from the sheer sweetness of it. "What's your name, son?"

"Billy," answered the young ballplayer.

"Very well, Billy, let's ask the Lord to forgive you and help you live a new life for Him."

*He sure is no preacher,* thought Billy. *He's got kind of a whiny voice.*

But as the colonel prayed, Billy could not keep the tears from pouring down his cheeks. "Dear Lord, Billy wants to tell You he's sorry for his sins; he believes You died on the cross for him. . . ."

*It must be You I'm hearing, Jesus. This must be Your voice.*

Billy entered the clubhouse for practice the next morning. He felt as if every inch of him was glowing like a firefly. *The boys will give it to me good today, but I don't care. I'm glad I went to the mission and found God.*

When Billy walked in, the usual loud banter ceased as if someone had given a signal. All of the White Stockings paused and turned as one man to stare at him. Billy took a deep breath, then smiled at his teammates. King Kelly walked deliberately across the room, leaned down to Billy, and held out his big hand.

"Billy, I'm proud of you! Religion is not my long suit," said the King, "but I'll help you all I can."[3] He shook hands with the amazed young ballplayer.

Cap Anson said nothing, but he clapped Billy on the back as he went to check on the equipment for the day's practice.

Fred Pfeffer, Jim Clarkson, the catcher "Silver" Flint, Jimmy McCormick, Tom Burns, Ned Williamson, and Abner Dalrymple all encouraged Billy.

Pfeffer, however, could not resist giving him a little dig. "Guess we all know you'll have to give up your wild, sinful ways, Billy," he said solemnly. The others hooted with laughter and really did not understand why Billy answered seriously, "Guess I will, Fred."

"Now, Jesus, we're askin' You to help Silas Wilson, whose horse ran away with him last week. Please help him get over his busted bones. Our missionaries need some help, too, Jesus. They're running short this month, as the pastor told us. . . ."

The girls in the Christian Endeavor group at Chicago's Jefferson Park Presbyterian Church barely suppressed a giggle. The leader, Mr. Watkins, sighed. God had blessed their young adults' group by sending them the energetic young man who loved Christ so passionately and spoke with Him so intimately. But he wouldn't mind if Billy would use an occasional "thee" or "thou."

The boy had professed new faith in Christ and joined the church in July. He had purchased a secondhand Bible for thirty-five cents and every week readied a list of questions about the scriptures to discuss with Watkins. Since his conversion, he had not missed a single service or Christian Endeavor meeting.

Watkins's glance fell on the tall, eighteen-year-old brunette with the luminous dark eyes who now led the testimony service. He looked back at Billy, who had not blinked since she had stood up. The leader shook his head slightly. Helen "Nell" Thompson was the only daughter of a well-to-do wholesale dairyman and ice cream manufacturer, a mature Christian girl who already taught Sunday school in her church. William Thompson, an iron-willed Scot who had served in the Civil War, would not take kindly to a ballplayer's interest in his daughter, even if he were an enthusiastic Christian.

*Father in heaven, keep that boy away from Nell,* prayed the youth leader. When the meeting ended, he made a beeline for Billy, intending to ask him some probing questions about his week's Bible reading.

But he need not have feared. Nell's steady beau, Archie Campbell, stuck to her like a burr. And when Billy tried to start a conversation with Nell, she adroitly steered her best friend, Sallie Morton, his way. Sallie, Watkins noted, captured the young man with ease, as she usually did. Before Billy knew what had happened, he was seeing the copper-haired Sallie home while Nell and Archie left for her home a block in the opposite direction.

Watkins breathed a sigh of relief. God in His wisdom usually managed these things better than he himself did. The youth leader raised a brief prayer of thanksgiving and called for some of the young men to help him rearrange the tables and chairs.

While Billy's spiritual life grew by leaps and bounds, his baseball career seemed to take a step back in 1886. Cap Anson called on Jimmy Ryan, a new outfielder with a superior throwing arm and a bat to match, to play the reserve outfielder role that Billy had held. Billy also fought a stubborn eye infection that affected his play throughout the latter part of the season. Cap used him very sparingly throughout 1886, though Billy retained a batting average of .243 and moved up to a ranking of tenth of thirty-three as a fielder.[4]

In a game with Detroit, he made the catch of his life.

Charley Bennett, Detroit's catcher, faced a full count from Chicago's pitcher Clarkson. When the pitcher slipped on the mound as he delivered the final pitch, Bennett slammed the low ball toward the home crowd.

Billy did not even stop to think *if* he could get the ball. He simply took off at a dead run as the ball whistled toward the crowd. "Get out of the way! Get out of the way!" yelled Billy. The fans parted, as he said, "Like the Red Sea for the rod of Moses."

"Oh, Lord," Billy prayed. "Oh, Lord, if You ever helped mortal man, help me to get that ball!"[5] He did, and the home crowd exploded with cheers!

Chicago finally edged past Detroit at the end of the season to take the National League pennant. The White Stockings played St. Louis once more in the World Series.

*The Series! I'd love to tell Nell that I did well in the best baseball games of the year. Maybe I'd even impress her father.*

Billy spent the entire time on the bench—and Chicago lost.

Soon, rumors flew about daily that Spalding planned major changes for his team.

*Wonder if he'll trade me.* Billy did not feel as close to Cap as he had before his conversion. *Maybe Cap is more upset by that than I thought. Maybe he won't stick up for me this time.* Billy knew that the Pittsburgh Alleghenies had expressed an interest in him. *Lord, I don't want to leave*

*Chicago. I don't want to leave my teammates and my church. I don't want to leave Nell. What will I do if they trade me, Lord? What will I do?*

Billy tried to still the butterflies in his stomach and poured himself more than ever into reading his Bible and activities at the Jefferson Park Presbyterian Church.

He even managed to corner Nell after the lone Christian Endeavor meeting that Archie could not attend.

"May I see you home, Miss Thompson?" he asked. It had taken weeks of determined evasion to convince Sallie of his lack of interest in her, and Billy was not going to miss his one chance to connect with Nell.

Nell laughed, then sighed. "All right, Mr. Sunday. Let me get my coat."

As they exited the church, Billy could see the lamps lit in Nell's beautiful home only a hundred yards away, but he headed around the block in the opposite direction.

"Mr. Sunday, my house is over there," insisted the young woman.

"But it is such a lovely night, Miss Thompson, and I do need the exercise," protested Billy lamely.

Nell looked at Billy and laughed again. Her younger brother, a mascot for the White Stockings, came home bursting with stories about Billy's fantastic catches, his incredible athletic prowess. She herself attended games and watched Billy run the bases like a deer and somersault in his efforts to catch the ball.

"Very well, Mr. Sunday, since you need exercise so much," agreed Nell, her brown eyes dancing.

After that night, Nell had talked to Billy more at church. Archie still saw her home after Christian Endeavor meetings, but Billy signed up for every church committee in which Nell was involved. He also walked past her house at least four times a day on his way to the ballpark. Her father wondered why Nell always seemed to be sweeping the front steps.

*I don't know what will come of it, Lord. Nell sees Archie. I'm still writing Clara. But I can't help but think You have plans for us together. That may not happen if they trade me to Pittsburgh.*

Billy did not have to wait long to find out. President A. G. Spalding had been so incensed by his team's loss in the World Series that he withdrew funds for their return travel expenses from St. Louis. The White Stockings had failed, he believed, because of their persistent drinking and partying. At the end of the regular season, Spalding had presented the team with his private detectives' reports of their activities. Billy, Anson, and a few others had passed Spalding's scrutiny, but he fined Kelly, Ryan, Flynn, McCormick, Flint, Gore, and Williamson each twenty-five dollars for breaking the team curfew and alcohol rules.

Spalding refused to believe that the White Stockings' resentment toward him might have played a part in their defeat in the World Series. Their lifestyles had cost him more than fifteen thousand dollars in gate receipts and had humiliated him personally and professionally. Spalding determined to "clean house."

First he fined five players two thousand dollars each because of their drinking violations. Then he sent fielder Abner Dalrymple and pitcher Jim McCormick to Pittsburgh and center fielder Gore to New York. But nothing stunned Chicago as his final sale did.

Spalding sold outfielder Mike "King" Kelly to his native Boston for a record price of ten thousand dollars. The King had played his most productive season ever, batting .388 and tallying 155 runs,[6] but Spalding believed he detracted from the respectable image he wanted to project. Let the Boston Beaneaters deal with the rowdy, arrogant star.

Billy Sunday and Jimmy Ryan were to take his place.

The newspapers trumpeted the shocking headlines. Chicago White Stocking fans alternately mourned the loss of Kelly and debated his replacements. Despite the differences in their lifestyles, Billy had always respected the King as a ballplayer; now he missed Kelly as his friend.

But Billy also breathed a prayer of thanks. *Well, Lord, looks like You want me in Chicago for the '87 season. But I'm goin' to need Your help a lot!*

# EIGHT

I t's a great day for a slide," said Billy, helping Nell onto the toboggan.

Cap Anson, ever ready to make money for his team, set up toboggan slides in the ballpark each winter. He still considered Billy far more trustworthy than any other ballplayer, so he asked him to take charge of the project. Billy had agreed, under one condition: Miss Nell Thompson was to enjoy all the free toboggan slides she wished!

He watched Nell zoom down the steep incline and slow to a stop. Then he hopped onto one of the sleds and took a rare free slide himself. When he slowed at the bottom, a ball of snow exploded in his face. Nell chortled wickedly at his yell of surprise and threw another one.

Billy grabbed a handful of snow, but he could not bring himself to hurl it. Mr. Pierce at the Davenport Soldiers' Home had considered throwing snowballs at girls akin to mortal sin. *Besides,* Billy mused, *I could never hit*

*Nell with anything, not even soft snow.* He reveled in the sparkling brown eyes, the thick dark curls that escaped Nell's red hat, the curve of her white cheek beneath the woolly matching scarf. *If only she would stop seeing Archie.*

Soon the holidays would arrive. Billy would go home to Iowa to work for the Northwestern Railway that winter. Clara still wrote Billy every week; Billy still wrote Clara. Why should he expect Nell to stop seeing Archie when he was planning to see Clara?

*I think I would give up anything for Nell if she would promise to marry me. But when I try to talk about us seriously, she always changes the subject.*

Billy was not yet ready to forget Clara's pert blue eyes and mischievous grin—at least, not until he knew how Nell really felt.

*I'll see how the winter goes,* he decided, watching Nell throw herself on the toboggan once more and slide joyously down the hill. *For now, it's just enough to watch her.*

Billy worked hard as a railroad fireman that winter. He visited his mother, who had married George Stowell. Jennie beamed with pride at the sight of her now-famous son; Billy noted with relief that his mother appeared well and reasonably happy.

He and Clara took sleigh rides with other couples over the snowy Iowa countryside. They went to taffy pulls, socials, and church gatherings.

*I always have a good time with Clara,* Billy thought. But Clara did not understand Billy's new passion for reading his Bible or talking about Christ to others.

*Clara's a good Christian girl,* he pondered, *but Nell's letters always bring me closer to God.*

"Nell! Over here, Nell!"

Billy dashed from the train, almost forgetting his suitcase. He wanted to sweep Nell into his arms and never let her go, but her mother stood smiling at her elbow. Mrs. Thompson, unlike her husband, had become Billy's friend and ally; she had written him often during his Iowa stay.

*Better not mess with that*, thought Billy. He dropped the valise and clasped both of Nell's hands tightly instead, locking his eyes on hers. Then Billy removed his hat and greeted Mrs. Thompson. He paused awkwardly. Nell still had said nothing.

"Perhaps Mr. Sunday would like to come to dinner, Nell," said the tall, elegant woman.

"He would be most welcome," said Nell.

*If she smiles at me like that one more time, I'll melt, Lord.* He gripped his hat, nearly crushing it. "I—I would love to come to dinner," said Billy.

Billy saw Nell more and more frequently. *Isn't she walking home from church with ol' Archie a lot less?* Billy wondered.

Much as Billy wanted to concentrate on Nell, he knew he must focus on baseball. The White Stockings would reunite in Chicago during the next few weeks, then travel to Hot Springs, Arkansas, once again for preseason training and games.

Billy would need to work on his batting in particular, because the rules had changed once more. The rules committee of 1887 had defined a strike zone for batters; no longer could a hitter call for a preferred high or low pitch. If a pitch was thrown over the plate between the batter's shoulders and knees, it would be called a strike. Spring training always meant new ways of doing things.

In 1887, it also meant many new faces on the White Stockings team. Spalding had retained the "Stone Wall" infield of Anson, Pfeffer, Williamson, and Burns, with the veteran Flint as catcher and the superb pitcher Clarkson. The outfield had shifted considerably. Rookies Marty Sullivan and Dell Darling joined Billy and Jimmy Ryan. Mark Baldwin took the place of Flynn, who had pitched and played outfield but sustained severe injuries at the end of the previous season. Tom "Tido" Daly backed up Silver Flint as catcher, and George "Rip" Van Haltren, a powerful batter, had been selected from Pittsburgh to replace McCormick as the White Stockings' second pitcher.

Anson viewed their preseason play with pleasure. They had all readily signed a complete abstinence pledge. Each day's practice ran smoothly, uninterrupted by prima donna tactics or hangovers. He particularly praised the outfield, saying his less-experienced lineup was as good as any other in the league.

*Now let them say I favor Billy just because he comes from Marshalltown*, Cap thought as he watched Billy field a nearly uncatchable ball.

Even exhibition games with St. Louis went well for Billy. He batted well and ran the bases cannily, once stealing second, third, and home to score a run during the series. He robbed a St. Louis player of a home run, determinedly diving for the ball, rolling over and over, clinging to it for dear life. Games in New York and other cities, as well as in Chicago, proved the same. The press predicted a great season for Kelly's replacement.

Things seemed to be going well with Nell, too. William Thompson continued to dislike Billy, but with Mrs. Thompson's support, he was allowed to make regular calls. Billy frequently accompanied the family to concerts and social events.

"Billy, I told Archie I do not want to see him any more," said Nell as she and Billy sat in the Thompson parlor after Sunday dinner.

Joy swelled Billy's heart until he thought it would explode from his chest, but her next words collapsed it.

"Do you care for Clara, Billy?"

Billy's usually ready tongue glued itself to his teeth, and he stared helplessly at her. Did he reek of the perfume from Clara's letter that he had read only this morning?

Nell rose. Cool and composed as a statue, she stood by the dark red velvet curtains. "If you think we may have a future together," she told him, "you must go to Iowa at once and tell Clara you no longer wish to see her."

"I—I. . ."

"If you leave soon, you will have time before the first game of the season," said Nell.

"I will, Nell! I will!"

A ghost of her usual rich smile flitted across her face. Nell turned and left the room.

"Billy, did you tell Clara about us?"

Billy twirled his hat miserably. "I did tell her, Nell. But I didn't see her. I just couldn't, Nell. I wrote a letter and sent it to her house."

Nell placed her hands on her hips and shook her head in amazement. "You went all the way to Iowa, and you never saw her?"

"No." Billy took the soft white hand in his. "But Nell, I did tell her about us. And I really believe that God is bringing us together."

He was working his little-boy magic on her, and Nell knew it, but she let him kiss her hand anyway.

"Then we will see what He has in store for us."

The promise of the 1887 season began to fade with the first games. The White Stockings as a team played poorly all through April. Billy struggled to bat and field consistently. He played a couple of spectacular games in May, making difficult catches on the run and hitting extremely well, including a home run. But during the next several games, Billy made some glaring fielding errors that caused the Chicago press to comment on the weakness of the new White Stockings outfield. Billy wrote Nell that a large, painful sore on his left hip had prevented him from playing his best, but he did not blame Cap Anson for benching him for a time or changing his position from center field to right field. "I'm just not playing my best right now," he wrote.

June brought improvement in Billy's game, especially his batting. Newspapers recorded an astonishing five triples and two home runs for Billy Sunday.[1] But his fielding errors caused some critics to insist that Dell Darling should be starting in right field.

Whether Billy was playing well or struggling, the Chicago crowds loved him. Even when the opposing team threw him out because he tried a risky steal, the fans absorbed his hunger as he strained every muscle to get to base. They cheered his wild, unorthodox attempts to make impossible catches. They lauded his novel way of sliding into base. Billy would leap in the air while still eight to ten feet from the bag and land sitting down with his feet on the bag, safe.

All agreed that Billy Sunday never bored them.

He improved every game until he injured his right ankle severely when he tried to steal a base. It would be more than a month before Billy would play again.

Despite his injury, Billy's reputation around the country had grown steadily. In August 1887, the *Boston Globe* took a survey to name the top base runner in the game. King Kelly took 413 votes; New York's Monte Ward received 147; and Billy rated third with 45 votes.[2]

When Billy returned in August to play in a game against Detroit, the home crowd welcomed him warmly.

*It's so good to run again, so good to see my friends, to hear the crowd yell for me. I really missed this ol' ballpark, Lord.*

Billy celebrated his return with two hits, crossing home plate himself once and bringing in two other runs.[3]

The White Stockings and Billy Sunday both endured unpredictable, difficult seasons. But the team finished third, with Detroit as league champion. Most Chicagoans felt third place to be quite acceptable, especially as the Boston team, which now listed the legendary King Kelly on its roster, placed fifth.

Spalding offered Billy a chance to play in California during off-season, but Billy declined because some games took place on Sundays.

Meanwhile, he expanded his spiritual horizons. He continued to serve actively at the Jefferson Park Presbyterian Church, including teaching a Sunday school class. Not long after his conversion, Billy also began systematic Bible study at Chicago's Young Men's Christian Association (YMCA), an organization that evangelized and taught Christian education to its converts. He attended theological seminars whenever he could. He began speaking to small groups of mesmerized boys at the "Y" in Chicago; before long, Billy also received invitations to speak to YMCA and church groups in other cities where he played baseball games.

Billy also managed to further his education. He studied English, physics, and elocution at the YMCA. While he could not qualify as a student at Northwestern University, he did take English, rhetoric, and history, as well as physiology and geography, at Evanston Academy, a prep school connected with the college, in exchange for coaching the Northwestern baseball team. He disliked math, yet forced himself to study it, sometimes astonishing others with his memory and ability to do calculations.

Despite his busy off-season schedule, Billy always made time for Nell. *Lots* of time.

"That boy is off in the clouds again," griped Cap Anson. His usually efficient assistant had made several errors in the team accounts, but Anson grinned as he complained.

Billy went home for Christmas, but before New Year's Day 1888, he boarded a train for Chicago. He prayed all the way back to his adopted hometown.

"Oh, Lord, please let Nell say yes. Please let her *father* say yes." Billy shivered as the frozen midwestern scenery flew past the window. The stern, bare trees and bleak fields posed a warmer welcome than the one he anticipated from Mr. Thompson.

When Billy exited the train, he filled his arms with red roses from a florist's shop and went straight to his sweetheart's door.

She opened it almost before he rang the bell.

Billy did not remember much about the encounter except that she said yes to his proposal. Nell said *yes!*

Nothing could pierce the euphoria that swirled around his head and filled him clear down to his toes, not even the inevitable interview with Mr. Thompson. The dour Scotsman snorted and raged like a perturbed bull. Why should he give his only daughter to a penniless ballplayer?

Not quite penniless, contradicted Billy. He had saved twelve hundred dollars of his 1887 salary.

He was a ballplayer who loved God with all his heart and tried to bring others to Christ, added Nell.

Thompson sputtered and growled, but his gracious wife defended the couple, and his sweet but iron-willed daughter made it clear she would not change her mind. Thompson gave his very reluctant consent.

Billy floated home to lie awake all night, seeing nothing but Nell's glowing eyes in the darkness.

*September 5, 1888. September 5, 1888.* He and Nell would be married on that date. *How can I wait that long?*

# NINE

Billy, you are a good man and a good player. The fans cheer you like nobody else," said A. G. Spalding. "You have a home here if you wish to stay."

Cap Anson nodded. Billy smiled at the man who had meant so much to him. Then his stomach double-knotted; Billy knew what was coming.

"But Pittsburgh has offered to pay you far more than we can afford," Spalding continued, "and you may have more opportunity to play there than here in Chicago."

Billy took a deep breath. "I need to talk it over with Nell," he said. "It's her future, as well as mine."

"Of course you'll want to discuss it with your young lady," agreed Spalding, smiling. He and Cap rose and shook Billy's hand.

"I'm so glad this happened *after* your father agreed to our marriage!" Billy exclaimed to Nell after the session. Even the thought of a temporary separation squeezed his heart painfully.

"Billy," said Nell, "we must pray together about this. But if it is an opportunity that God has sent, you must accept it."

"But it would mean our being apart until September. We would move far away from your parents, our church, and all our friends. Do you really want to do that?"

"It would be so hard to stay here while you live in Pittsburgh! And I would miss them all terribly, Billy." She smoothed his hair gently. "But soon we'll be together for the rest of our lives." Nell smiled, then sighed. "And we must be practical." The two discussed Billy's limited playing time and their meager finances, then agreed to pray for a week about the matter.

Nell's father struggled with their conclusion; the parent in him longed for his daughter's immediate presence, but the Christian businessman respected their down-to-earth reasoning.

Billy contacted the Pittsburgh Alleghenies and told them he would accept their generous offer.

Billy surveyed his new team. Abner Dalrymple, an outfielder whom Chicago had traded earlier to Pittsburgh, tossed the ball to him. Billy threw it to John Coleman, the other starting outfielder. Abner had welcomed him with open arms. He and his wife insisted that Billy stay with them when he first arrived in Pittsburgh, an arrangement that did much to assuage Billy's loneliness.

*It was tough, Lord, leaving Chicago. Cap brought all the boys to the station to say good-bye to me. Even a bunch of fans showed up. I didn't think I could let go of Nell, but You helped me. I hated riding that train alone, Lord.* Billy had tried not to remember the long-ago heartbreak of leaving his mother at the Ames train station, the agony of the journey to the Glenwood orphanage.

But this trip was different. Billy read his Bible by the hour as the train chugged eastward. He clutched the lace handkerchief that Nell had slipped into his hand before he boarded the train, and he prayed for their future together.

As the train entered the outskirts of Pittsburgh, his spirits rose. For the first time in his baseball career, Billy Sunday would start as outfielder. He would work with people like future Hall of Famer James "Pud" Galvin, or "Gentle Jeems," whose merciless pitching seemed to contradict his mild appearance. Jake Beckley, a rookie who also was elected to the Hall of Fame later in his career, was already astounding his fellow players with his exciting fielding and batting. Catcher George "Doggie" Miller, a fan favorite, made Billy feel at home immediately.

*The Alleghenies sure aren't the White Stockings*, Billy admitted to himself. The shabby, aging Pittsburgh stadium did not resemble Chicago's luxurious one in the least. The Fort Wayne Railroad tracks near it actually formed its outfield boundary. The Alleghenies had placed sixth of eight in their league.[1] Horace Phillips, the Pittsburgh manager, had struggled to unite a team beset with drinking problems. He did not seem to have Cap Anson's gifts of inspiration, organization, and education.

*But he knows baseball. I'll say that for him*, Billy thought. Phillips had already made some valuable suggestions that helped his batting.

With the exit of unstable players and the advent of talented, clean-living ones like Billy Sunday, Pittsburgh president W. A. Nimick hoped to rebuild his sagging team.

Billy chased a powerfully hit practice grounder and

grabbed it moments before a whistling locomotive thundered down the railroad tracks. He hurled it to Doggie Miller at home plate. The catcher grinned and gave him a "thumbs-up" sign.

*Please make this the best season I've ever had, Lord. And make it go fast!*

Billy and the Alleghenies faced a formidable opponent in their first home game on April 20, 1888: Detroit, the past year's National League pennant winner. His palms sweated as he clutched the bat. *Lord, help me. Make them glad they brought me to Pittsburgh.*

Billy brought the screaming home crowd to its feet as he stole three bases and scored two runs.[2]

Although the Alleghenies could not handle the Chicago White Stockings a week later and lost 7–2, Billy played well against his old team, connecting on four of five attempts at bat and scoring both of Pittsburgh's runs.[3] Later, when Detroit overwhelmed his team in a four-game series, Billy fielded, batted, and ran well. He scored the Alleghenies' only run in two of the contests.[4] As Pittsburgh slumped, Billy continued to play well. He even stole a base off Mike Kelly in a series against Boston, bringing down the house. He continued to play wonderfully against Washington, Indianapolis, New York, and other teams. He struggled midseason in his batting but remained consistent in his fielding, and soon his hitting improved. Then he sprained his ankle once more and missed several games, but he came back stronger than ever to play in a series against Chicago.

Cap Anson shifted uneasily in his seat in the clubhouse. His team was behind, and Billy Sunday grinned at him from third base. Anson hardly glanced at him; he knew all too well the fierce focus of those blue eyes, the determination that inevitably resulted in a score. *Hope the boys remember what we practiced. If Billy's on third, fake a throw elsewhere, then get it to third to tag him out.*

The next Pittsburgh batter connected lightly, and the White Stocking pitcher grabbed the ball and aimed for second base. Billy took off in a twinkling, duped by the ruse, but the pitcher threw off-balance, and the ball sailed over the third baseman's head. Billy joyously crossed home plate as his teammates celebrated. Pittsburgh defeated Chicago 8–7.[5]

In Chicago newsrooms, bars, and neighborhoods, baseball fans pondered the possibilities. Pittsburgh fans anxiously debated the future of their center fielder. Had the White Stockings "loaned" Billy Sunday to Pittsburgh just so everyone could see that Cap Anson had not practiced favoritism in wanting to retain the outfielder? Would Billy return at the end of the season to wear a White Stockings uniform once more?

Other rumors sent Billy into a rage. One Chicago newspaper speculated Billy would shortly marry his Iowa sweetheart. He lost no time in contacting the paper, which printed a correction stating that Billy planned to marry Miss Thompson of Chicago.

"It was just a mistake, Billy," cajoled Nell. She had begun to regard the story with some amusement and wanted to spend their brief time together more positively.

For once, Billy's sense of humor was missing. "I don't care what they print about me, Nell. But when it comes to *us*, I'm not going to stand for it."

All too soon, Billy had to board the train to Pittsburgh with his team.

"It won't be long, Billy!"

"Not soon enough, Nell." He kissed her lingeringly, turning his back on three reporters who scratched on their writing pads from a respectful distance.

Once more Billy had to content himself with writing long letters to Nell. Some numbered almost fifty pages! "Really, they contained nothing but variations of 'I'm so lonesome!' " laughed Nell later.[6] Although Billy wrote that his Pittsburgh teammates indulged in the usual drinking, gambling, and carousing, he boycotted anything connected with bars or wild ways. "I love you, Nell, and I'll always be faithful to you," he assured his bride-to-be.

The newspapers reported that Billy had immediately begun to attend local churches. Soon he volunteered to teach a class of amazed young men, who besieged him with baseball questions.

"How do you know when to steal, Billy?" asked a wiry, black-haired teenager.

"Yeah, how many bases have you stolen this season?" inquired his stocky, sandy-haired friend.

Billy replied, as he had many times, that he would be glad to answer their baseball questions the next day, "but I can't do it today. This is God's day, and I am here to do His work the best I know how, so let us see what we can get out of this lesson."[7]

The boys sighed and shuffled the pages of their Bibles, but they soon lost themselves in the baseball player's colorful, inventive instruction.

The YMCA, well acquainted with Billy's connections in Chicago, invited him to speak often, as did area churches. When the Alleghenies played elsewhere, Billy packed his free time with speaking engagements and often visited YMCAs and missions. Reporters followed him everywhere; they had written reams about wild, dissipated baseball players. This likable young man who lived his faith so openly presented a curious contrast.

"Where you going today, Billy?" asked one writer as he followed the baseball player and his friend Jerry McAuley to a waiting carriage on the bustling streets of New York City.

"We're headed downtown to Jerry's mission, Al," Billy told him. "Why don't you boys come along?"

"I never been to a mission before," said Al's co-worker uneasily. "Will we have to listen to preaching?"

"If we do, it won't be boring, Ernie," answered Al. "Come on, the boss said we gotta get this story."

The two found themselves sitting on rude benches near Billy, hemmed in by derelicts who reeked of alcohol, sweat, and urine.

Al nonchalantly scribbled a note or two, trying not to show his fear. As a reporter, he had entered rough places, but this mission surpassed them all. He dared not look at Ernie.

A small choir of unkempt men entered and began singing. Al winced. *That fella in the front sounds like gravel shook in a bucket.* Nevertheless, the reporter strained his ears to listen. Why did he want to hear? What were they singing?

"Jesus loves me, this I know, for the Bible tells me so. . . ," sang the men.

*I'm a worse singer than that gravel guy.* But Al hummed along.

"Yes, Jesus loves me, yes, Jesus loves me," sang the ragged choir.

Al stole a look at Billy Sunday. The dapper young professional ballplayer was weeping unashamedly.

"The Bible tells me so."

*Can't cry.* Al surreptitiously wiped his eyes on his coat sleeve.

*Thank God, Jerry's taking the floor. Hopefully we'll have a nice dull sermon, and I can get out of here.*

But Jerry introduced Billy Sunday, who rose from his seat and began, "Say, boys, did your mother ever sing you songs like that? Mine did."

Al and Ernie squirmed in their seats. The huge, ox-like creature on Ernie's right glared at him. Ernie sat very still.

"A few years ago, it was music like that that reminded me of how much Jesus loves me. He loves you, too, even if you're the worst sinner on this earth. Even if you can't wait to get out of here. . . ."

Al felt cold sweat dribble down his back. *It's gonna be a long afternoon.*

At the end of the service, Billy prayed with several men who had come forward, then shook hands heartily. He even hugged several of the dirtiest tramps. Al shook his head in disbelief, but he waited respectfully until Billy could speak with him.

"Billy, what are you doing?" asked Ernie when the room had emptied. "You're a professional baseball player. You don't have to be here with a bunch of down-and-outers."

"Jesus is God, and He didn't have to die on a cross for me, either," said Billy.

Al shook his head slightly at Ernie. "Thanks, Billy, for inviting us along. It was. . .interesting."

Billy chuckled. "It's always interesting where God is working."

"Hey, Billy, what's the matter with you?"

His teammates grinned. They knew why he leaped into the air like a frog for every catch, why he danced on the bases as if they were red-hot. Billy even turned a few flips for the crowd between innings without a word of reproof from the manager, Phillips.

"That boy's got it bad," he said, shaking his head, smiling.

All the Alleghenies knew this game at Indianapolis was Billy's last before he boarded a train to Chicago. Tonight he would meet Nell at the station, and tomorrow, September 5, 1888, they would finally marry.

*These six months have dragged by like a stubborn old mule, Lord. But now they're over and done with!*

Billy finished his game and rushed to the train station. As he rode through the rich, ripening cornfields of Indiana, his heart sang a private hymn of praise in rhythm with the chuffing of the steam engine.

*Thank-You-thank-You-thank-You-Lord.*

# TEN

I, William Ashley Sunday, take thee, Helen Amelia Thompson, to be my lawfully wedded wife," said Billy. Nell, elegant in her shimmering steel gray silk dress, smiled, and Billy almost forgot his next lines.

*Oh, Nell, I thought I loved you before, but I think I'm going to burst before this is over.* Billy's best man, Fred Pfeffer from the Chicago White Stockings, had had to nudge him with Nell's wedding ring before Billy remembered to place it on her finger. The wedding guests seated in the Thompsons' flower-decked parlor smiled, knowing protocol was not Billy's strong point.

Finally Dr. David Marquis of the McCormick Theological Seminary pronounced the couple man and wife. The Thompsons had prepared an afternoon tea for everyone. Billy watched Nell drink tea from the corner of his eye, her long, slim fingers poised on the teacup's handle, the afternoon sun playing in her dark hair. Billy enjoyed seeing friends he had missed while he played baseball in Pittsburgh, but the real celebration awaited the newlyweds elsewhere.

A. G. Spalding had reserved a private box for Billy and Nell at the White Stockings' late-afternoon game. At their arrival, the crowd rose and cheered joyously. The White Stockings all bowed, taking off their caps to the new couple. Mr. and Mrs. Sunday waved back, Nell enjoying the fun as much as Billy.

When the game ended, the couple said good-bye to the Thompsons and other well-wishers at the train station and took the *Pennsylvania Limited* to Pittsburgh. Even something as important as a wedding could not change the Alleghenies' baseball schedule. The very next day, Billy appeared in the outfield at the rickety old stadium in Pittsburgh. His teammates surprised them with a special welcome and gifts: a bronze clock that the Sundays cherished all their married life, a heavy sideboard, a desk, wedding china, and silverware.

"Well, Nell, we're home for a few days, then we're off to Boston again with the team. Do you mind?"

Nell laughed. "I'd like to get things a little settled," she said, "but I've had to stay put while you've traveled all over. Now I get to go!"

Billy thought gratefully of the large monetary gift his father-in-law had pressed into his hand before their wedding. "We want you two to travel together. That's important, especially when you're first married," said William Thompson. It was the longest and certainly the most positive conversation Billy had had with the man. *Maybe he's beginning to see that I really do love God and I love his daughter*, thought Billy.

Boston, New York, Detroit, Philadelphia, Indianapolis,

Washington, then Chicago again—Nell loved them all. The adventurous couple thrived on their exciting new life. They liked staying in hotels, trying new restaurants, seeing the sights together. In the midst of his unpredictable lifestyle, Billy experienced a sense of stability he never had before, because Nell stayed close to his side. She cheered him at the games, consoled him when he lost or made bad plays, and managed their schedule and money so capably that Billy never had to concern himself with such things. For the next forty-seven years, Nell would make Billy's world a safer, warmer place.

"If I had known it was going to be this good," Billy told his wife, "I would have married you and taken you to Pittsburgh right off, instead of waiting six months!"

Not only had God blessed Billy with the love of his life, He granted him his best season ever. Billy stole seventy-one bases in 1888; he might have led his league if he had not injured his ankle midseason. *Spalding's Guide,* a noted baseball magazine, rated him seventh as a fielder in his league, while others declared he was the best. Billy played as many games in his first year at Pittsburgh—120—as he had the previous three years combined in Chicago. The consistency sharpened his skills considerably, which built his confidence. Although his batting average remained mediocre (.236), Billy placed at the top of the team roster in scoring runs.[1]

The Alleghenies progressed, experiencing their first winning season in years, although they once again placed sixth in their league.

Pittsburgh president W. A. Nimick mentally predicted a better season the next year. He and Pittsburgh fans ended the baseball season with a novel sense of optimism.

A. G. Spalding, impressed by Billy's first year in Pittsburgh, contacted him about playing on an all-star team he was recruiting to take on the road with his White Stockings during the off-season. He even spoke of traveling in Europe and Australia.

"Oh, Billy! I would love to see the world!" Nell's dark eyes shone.

Billy nodded, his own face beaming with anticipation. "But Nell, remember my knee."

Nell nodded, her expression clouding. Billy had torn a ligament in his knee during the last part of the season and still could not walk without a limp.

"Why don't we see what the doctor says?" suggested Nell. Billy had consulted President Garfield's own physician in Washington, D.C., and he had strictly limited the ballplayer's physical activity. After another appointment, Billy was forced to decline Spalding's offer. "If you play on that knee this winter," the physician had declared, "you may have to give up baseball for good."

"It's all right," insisted Nell. "I would have loved to travel overseas, but this means we can go home to Chicago for the winter."

Billy swallowed his disappointment when he saw the eager spark in his wife's eyes. "You've been such a good sport, Nell. All those endless train trips with my rowdy teammates. All the miles far away from your mother and father. I'm glad you will be able to spend time with your family."

"Yes, and the YMCA will certainly be happy to see you, Billy," said Nell, hugging him.

Billy thought of ministering at the Pacific Garden Mission, speaking to groups of awestruck boys at the Chicago "Y," taking Bible courses with old friends there.

He would probably coach the Northwestern University baseball team again, but baseball would not dominate his life as it did during the regular season; instead, ministry would.

*I love doing God's work.* Suddenly Billy realized that, deep down, he felt relief at the way God had closed the door to his all-star trip.

He turned to Nell and tweaked her nose. "So, Mrs. Ex–World Traveler, when do we head for home?"

The Sundays spent a delightful winter in Chicago, living near the Thompsons. To their great joy, William and Billy became good friends. Nell's father evidently had decided that Billy's conversion and devotion to his daughter were genuine. His young son-in-law, who had never experienced the affection and wisdom of a father, grew to love the irascible but caring Scot.

The Chicago social scene welcomed young Mr. and Mrs. Sunday with open arms; hostesses all around town invited the handsome, vibrant couple to their balls and dinners.

"Look at those two," whispered Chicago gossips. "After a few months, most young married couples are only too happy to mingle with others. He never lets go of her hand, as if they were still courting."

Nell threw herself into volunteer work at the Jefferson Park Presbyterian Church, which had sorely missed her. Billy coached the college boys, teaching them Christian values as well as baseball tips.

*Maybe, Lord, I can help them escape the things that have wrecked my pro baseball friends' lives.*

How Billy loved talking with the little boys who crowded around him at the YMCA!

"Mr. Sunday, when are you comin' back to Chicago to play?"

"Why ain't you a pitcher, Mr. Sunday?"

"Mr. Sunday, how can I be the best baseball player in the world, like you?"

Billy answered their baseball questions with a straight face, but their theological ones sometimes sent him, coughing violently, into another room, where he laughed until he could once more maintain his composure.

"Mr. Sunday, why did God invent baseball?"

"Did you change your name to Sunday after you got to be a Christian?"

"If God's your best friend, why doesn't He help you bat better?"

Most of all, Billy loved working the "tenderloin" section of Chicago, the miserable slums where despairing ghosts of men and women haunted the streets, living a nightmare existence. Bleary-eyed alcoholics stared at the clean-cut young ballplayer as he invited them to Pacific Garden Mission for a hot meal. Prostitutes simpered and beckoned, but Billy looked at them with compassion and shared the gospel with them. Sometimes saloons emptied as disbelieving patrons sought autographs from their favorite base stealer.

*Lord, they're just like pitiful lost animals, with no one to care for them. Please bring them home to You.*

"Billy, you're a natural," said the YMCA director. "God uses you to lead people to Himself. Have you ever considered full-time Christian service?"

Billy slowly gathered his Bible-study materials. "I've thought about it," he answered. "But I have a contract with the Alleghenies for two more years."

"God is bigger than any contract," answered the

director. "If you do consider it, please contact me. I'd love to have a man like you on our team."

"I'll pray about it," said Billy Sunday.

"Good-byes are never fun," said Billy as he and Nell boarded the train to Pittsburgh.

"Of course not," she answered, trying not to let the tears flow as she waved to her parents. "But at least we're saying them together."

Billy held her close. "What would I do without you, Nell?"

He would need her love and support during the 1889 season.

Unrest swept into baseball stadiums, where owners enjoyed ever-increasing receipts. Many baseball players resented their prosperity, wanting a larger share of the profits. Billy, remembering his Marshalltown days, thanked God every day for an adequate salary and travel expenses, but several of his teammates succumbed to the gold fever; they played with little enthusiasm or skill.

Billy's Battle of the Bat began once more. Special instructors tutored him. He gave it his all, studying the experts, practicing long hours, doing anything he could to increase his batting average.

Instead, it went down.

*Well, God, we can't all be tops. I'm just glad You're there when I feel like the worst ballplayer in the world.*

Although Billy and his team struggled in 1889, his spiritual life continued to grow. He found himself ministering more and more at home and as he traveled, speaking to men's groups and young people's organizations, especially those tied to the YMCA.

"Those classes back at Evanston and the Y have really

helped you, Billy. You improve each time you speak," encouraged Nell.

Billy nodded his thanks and pondered: *Just what do you have in mind for me, Lord?*

The 1889 season proved difficult for other reasons. He and Nell were now expecting their first child, and she could no longer accompany him as she had during their first carefree year. They also needed to save their money. "Babies sure need a lot of stuff," Billy said proudly.

Little Helen arrived in January 1890, brightening her parents' lives with her smiles and coos.

*Thank You, God, for my family. Even when life is tough, I just hold my girls and know how good You are.*

The Philadelphia Phillies approached Pittsburgh with an offer for Billy; he signed a contract to play for them from 1891–1893.

The 1890 baseball season exploded when most of the players created their own Players League. Many cities faced the prospect of supporting two major-league teams, which few could afford. All of the Pittsburgh Alleghenies joined the Players League, leaving only Bill Sowders, a third-string pitcher, and Billy Sunday.

Despite Nell's thrifty management, Billy and Nell struggled with debt. Billy sympathized with his fellow players, but he disliked the money-hungry attitudes they projected to the world. He decided to remain with the Pittsburgh Alleghenies' organization. He did not want to join the "Pittsburgh Pirates," the Players League group, so nicknamed because of their salary negotiating techniques.

Billy began the nightmare 1890 season, playing with minor-league players hastily gathered by the Alleghenies' association.

*I can't believe they're making me pitch today, Lord. I didn't even pitch in Marshalltown.*

Billy's pitching career did not last long. He walked one batter, then one tripled and another doubled. He hurled a fast ball at the next man, striking him so hard in the leg, he limped to first base. Phillips mercifully sent in Sowders to relieve Billy, and he trudged back to the outfield, where he belonged.

Even the most loyal Pittsburgh fans soon sought other entertainment after watching their team lose twenty-three games in a row. The Alleghenies lost a total of 113 games in 1890.[2]

"Hey, Sunday, do you make your wife come to the games?" asked one of his teammates. "She's here every time."

Nell waved at her husband from the empty stands as if she would not think of being elsewhere. She held up baby Helen, who grinned at her daddy.

"If all the wives and children came, we might fill up half a section," said Billy. He counted the fans once more—eighteen, nineteen, twenty. A total of twenty people had shown up to watch the game.

Billy chased balls with his usual vigor and easily hit a double off the minor-league pitcher on the other team, but he could not wait to leave the dilapidated ball field.

Eventually the Players League experienced such severe financial problems that the ballplayers negotiated with their former owners and returned to their respective teams. Billy welcomed them with relief; once more he could work with talented, skilled teammates.

*But I'm not happy playing professional ball anymore, Lord. I'm just not.*

Billy and Nell prayed together fervently. Invitations

to speak crowded his schedule so that he had little time to focus on baseball. Billy felt himself drawn more and more to the spiritual needs of the people around him. The Chicago YMCA once more extended an invitation to minister with its organization. Billy talked with the Phillies' owners about his desire to pursue full-time Christian ministry. They lauded his noble ambitions, but wanted Billy to play with their club. He was to report on April 1.

"Nell, I do believe that God wants me to work with the Y. But there's still the contract with the Phillies. I can't believe God would want me to do anything dishonorable. I signed the contract; I'll follow through unless God makes a way for my release. If the Phillies do not release me by March 25, I will play for them as planned."

Billy received his release on March 15.

He would soon begin his work as the Chicago YMCA's religious director for a yearly salary of one thousand dollars.

When other teams learned of Billy's release, several immediately expressed interest in him. Cincinnati offered him a salary of five thousand dollars for 1891 alone. Some Christian businessmen, knowing of the young family's financial needs, urged Billy to play that summer, then begin work in the fall.

Nell would have none of it.

"We do not need to think about this," she told Billy. "You promised God you would stop playing pro baseball."

He refused the offers. Billy, Nell, and baby Helen said good-bye to their friends in Pittsburgh and boarded a train for Chicago.

# ELEVEN

"Nell, I wish you could have seen God work this morning," Billy told his wife excitedly. "Old Lem Sanders showed up at the Pacific Garden Mission and decided to ask Christ into his life!"

"Lem? But I thought even Colonel Clark thought he might never change," said Nell, wiping food from her small son's mouth as he howled his protests. "That's incredible news, Billy!" She released him with a pat, and little George toddled to his father.

"I guess God can even outguess Colonel Clark," said Billy, wrestling with the little boy.

Nell smiled to see him so happy. It was a welcome change from the frustration her husband had fought frequently the past year.

Billy loved the evangelistic part of his YMCA job. Day after day he patrolled the ugliest parts of Chicago, hanging around outside saloons so he could talk with the homeless alcoholics, thieves, prostitutes, drug addicts, and gamblers who frequented the taverns, urging them to abandon the miserable lives they led. Twice he encountered childhood friends from Iowa who wanted to sample life in the big city. Billy warned them to avoid the hell in the Chicago "tenderloin" and the one to come.

"Jesus Christ loves you," he told anyone who would listen. "He wants to help you out of this mess and save you from hell. He can do it, too. Come with me to the Y or the Garden Mission."

Nothing made Billy's day, Nell knew, like rescuing lonely, brokenhearted people.

Nothing infuriated him as much as office work.

Billy had performed administrative duties well since his days with Cap Anson. He did not mind making travel arrangements or handling money. But Billy had also spent much of his time running, jumping, throwing, and batting outdoors. During his eight years as a professional ballplayer, he had traveled incessantly, seeing new, exciting places, hearing the roar of stadium crowds.

Now his cramped YMCA office imprisoned him for endless hours as he raised funds, contacted churches, and organized meetings. Nell had heard his supervisors speak enthusiastically of Billy's hard work and dedication.

*But he can't sit still much better than George,* sighed Nell. She always had enjoyed Billy's boundless energy, but at times she wondered if her husband would explode from sheer rage. Billy had struggled somewhat with insomnia in the past, but now Nell heard him rise frequently at night to pace in their tiny parlor.

The Sunday family had also suffered financially. She had made the $83.33 per month salary stretch before George was born, but now even her careful management could not make it cover their expenses. Nell knew Billy skipped lunches at times so there would be more at home, even though he denied it vehemently, and only she realized how much style-conscious Billy hated wearing cheap celluloid collars to save laundry costs.

Various professional baseball teams had made tempting offers to Billy, but he steadfastly refused them all. Nell nodded in agreement as she washed the dishes. They both knew he had made the right decision; Billy belonged in full-time Christian work.

"Yet, Lord," Nell prayed as she scrubbed the dirty pans, "I can't believe You made Billy to sit in an office the rest of his life." She wiped her hands and bowed her head. "Please, Lord, give him work to do that will bless him, as well as others."

In 1894 the Sundays received a letter from Dr. J. Wilbur Chapman, a prominent Philadelphia pastor and evangelist. Billy had met him through their close mutual friend, Peter Bilhorn, who often sang at Chapman's meetings.

"You have to see this man to believe him," Peter had told Dr. Chapman, and after hearing Billy speak at a YMCA meeting, Chapman knew he had found the man to assist him in his new endeavor. Chapman planned extensive tent meeting campaigns throughout the Midwest, and he needed an "advance man" to raise his tent, initiate local support, gather a choir, and speak at pre-crusade meetings in churches, shops, and factories.

"You will also sell my books, line up committees, and preach when I am unable," proposed the evangelist. "I will pay you forty dollars per week, if you are interested."

Billy read the letter aloud to Nell after they rocked Helen and George to sleep. He stood at the bedroom door watching the tiny, peaceful faces. "It would mean my being gone for long periods of time," he said. "You would be alone much of the time."

"I wouldn't be alone, Billy." She stroked his cheek. "Mother and Father live so close by, and all our friends."

"But I'll miss you, Nell." He folded her into his arms.

"I know."

They stood silently for a few moments. *He will miss me? Sounds like Billy's already made up his mind.* But deep down, Nell sensed the letter was an answer to her prayers. She pulled back to see her husband's eyes shining with mingled joy and pain.

"Billy, you must do what God wants you to do," she said. "Let's pray together for a few days about it, then let the Y and Dr. Chapman know."

*I feel as if I've been let out of a cage.* Billy loved walking to the end of a train car and standing outside, feeling the wind blow through his thick hair. Since he had gone to work for Dr. Chapman, he could not seem to get enough of the landscapes and towns rushing past train windows, the *chuff-chuff* of train engines, the blast of the whistles. He enjoyed meeting Christians in Terre Haute, Indiana; Oskaloosa, Iowa; and Troy, New York. He had even met Benjamin Harrison at an Indianapolis meeting when Chapman had sent him to invite the former president to join him on the platform. Every day was an adventure for Billy as he organized campaigns for the bespectacled, scholarly looking evangelist.

Not an intellectual himself, Billy marveled that the man preached the gospel so effectively to everyday audiences. Chapman, a veteran of earlier crusades along the eastern seaboard and overseas, pioneered techniques that would influence not only his new assistant, but mass evangelism in the United States throughout following years. He was an excellent administrator and business-man, one of the first revivalists to plan precrusade publicity, financial arrangements, area church support, and recruitment of local workers.

Billy studied Chapman's oratorical methods closely. At first he felt uneasy about speaking as a substitute for the evangelist, but congregations in tents, halls, and opera houses welcomed him enthusiastically. Large audiences of men, in particular, gathered to hear Billy because of his baseball past.

Although Billy loved the challenges of his new career, he missed Nell and the children deeply. He always rejoiced when Chapman accepted revivals near Chicago or took vacations around the holidays. Billy took the first train home whenever he could.

*It's a good thing You keep me mighty busy, Lord. If I had time to really think about Nell and the children, I don't think I could stand it.*

Christmas 1895 approached quickly. Billy sought the biggest and prettiest doll he could find for Helen, who was nearly six years old.

*Every time I've come home, George is doing something new and exciting. Although I hope it's not quite as exciting as the last time.* When Billy had come home during the fall, he and Nell had had to organize a search party for George, who had disappeared while his mother bartered with a grocer. They found their son three blocks away, on his way to the park.

Billy chuckled and shook his head in dismay. *What will keep him busy for a few minutes so Nell can have some peace?* Even George's calm mother sometimes wearied of his energy.

Billy bought a large red rubber ball. He promised himself he would also buy a sled when he got to Chicago. Maybe Cap still ran the toboggan slide in the stadium.

*I'm gone an awful lot. But at least Helen and George have a daddy alive who can play with them.*

"Here's a letter from Dr. Chapman," observed Billy.

"Don't read it now," entreated Nell. "We've had such a wonderful Christmas; I want it to last a little longer. It's only the twenty-sixth. Can't we forget your work just for tonight? You can open it in the morning." She snuggled close to her husband. Her dark eyes shown in the soft lamplight.

"Sure," agreed Billy, tossing the letter on the desk. "Whatever you say, Nell."

They turned the gas lights off and watched the feathery snowflakes blanket the bleak Chicago street below.

"Nell."

At Billy's tone, she turned sharply. "What's wrong, Billy?"

He tried to smile. "Well, I don't know if it's wrong, exactly. But it'll sure be different."

Nell poured maple syrup on Helen's pancakes, then grasped the letter while Billy held George.

Dr. Chapman was writing to inform Billy that his former church in Philadelphia had contacted him about resuming the pastorate once more. He had decided to accept and would assume his new position on January 1, 1896. Dr. Chapman had enjoyed working with Billy very much and would be glad to recommend him highly to any future employers.

Nell gave a small sob, then a laugh. Billy pulled her to

him. "God will work this out," he told her. "But you may have to get used to my hanging around here for a while."

"Where on earth is Garner, Iowa?" City-born Nell had had little experience with small towns.

Billy chuckled. "I think it's about seventy-five miles north of Ames. Guess I'll find out where it is." Only a few days after Chapman had informed Billy of his decision to return to Philadelphia, another letter had arrived. Dr. Chapman had recommended Billy for a ten-day revival that three Garner churches hoped to hold in January in their local opera house.

"Only thing is, I put together just eight sermons to preach when I needed to substitute for Chapman," said Billy half-jokingly. "Where am I going to find two more?"

Nell looked straight at him. "Billy," she said, "if God wants you to hold a ten-day revival in Garner, He'll give you the other two."

"I am so glad that Jesus loves me, Jesus loves me, Jesus loves me. . . ."

As Billy waved his arm to keep time, he thanked God he had learned a little about directing music from his friend Peter Bilhorn.

*I didn't realize I'd have to preach* and *direct the music for this revival!* Billy "didn't know a note from a horsefly," but he willingly "supplied the vim, ginger, and tabasco sauce!"[1]

Fortunately, the twenty-voice choir sang with plenty of enthusiasm, although one high soprano grated on even Billy's untrained ear. The congregation, composed of farmers and Garner's storekeepers, also confidently joined in, and Billy gave a sigh of relief when the song service ended.

His voice shook a little as he began, but Billy soon warmed to the gathering, which reminded him of get-togethers of friends and family in Marshalltown and Ames. The tanned, honest-faced farmers and their sturdy wives and hordes of children made him feel right at home. He did not remember much of what he said later, but attendance grew steadily throughout the meetings, and the town newspaper printed positive accounts of the revival.

To Billy's great joy, many came to Christ, including one of the richest men in Hancock County. He told Billy he had refused to become a Christian twenty-one years before at a Dwight L. Moody revival, but now the man blinked back tears as Billy prayed with him.

The grateful Garner churches took up a collection the last day of the campaign and paid Billy sixty-eight dollars.

Before he left Garner, a letter arrived from Sigourney, Iowa, in the southeast portion of the state. Would Billy consent to holding a revival there?

He would. Billy traveled to Sigourney, arriving at the town's largest church, where the meetings were to be held. To his amazement, worshipers occupied every seat in the building, and men, women, and children filled the aisles.

*Well, Lord, maybe Garner went better than I thought it did.*

The choir members who filled the loft burst into song, led by John Van Winkle from Keota, whom Billy had hired.

*Thank You, Lord, for leading me to John. You know even better than I do that I'm no singer.*

Billy preached his sermon, "Whatsoever Ye Sow, That Shall Ye Reap." As usual, he spoke without mincing words. "When I am through," he would soon tell congregations across the country, "you needn't appoint a committee to find out what I am talking about."[2] Sin was sin. God offered people a chance to repent and believe in His Son, Jesus Christ, who died for their sins. If they refused God's invitation, they should expect to live in hell forever. Somehow, Billy's down-to-earth style, his folksy anecdotes, his knowledge of plows and planting seasons connected him to his audience. They held their breath as they watched the athletic young speaker move incessantly; he paced, gestured, and even slid into imaginary bases to prove his point.

At the end of each service, Billy invited his listeners to come forward to ask Christ to change their lives. They responded by clogging the altar area every night. Billy counseled, shook hands, and slapped shoulders, talking with new believers late into the night. He and Van Winkle distributed hundreds of conversion cards to them, following Dr. Chapman's innovative practice. These affirmed the signer's resolve to put his faith in Jesus Christ and live a productive Christian life. They also provided Billy with valuable information such as name, address, and which church the new convert wished to attend. The local newspapers likened Billy to Dwight L. Moody and lauded him as imaginative, provocative, and effective. At the end of the revival, the people in Sigourney voted to retain Billy for more meetings.

"Not a single dissenting vote," said the pastor to Billy. "Please, Mr. Sunday. You have blessed us beyond measure, and we need to hear more."

Billy had to decline because he had already agreed to hold meetings in Pawnee, Nebraska. This scenario repeated itself frequently, with Billy regretfully telling his admirers "no" because of schedule conflicts. In reality, he later confessed, Billy probably could have remained in town for a few extra days, but during his early ministry, he exhausted his supply of sermons with one campaign.

Before the Pawnee City campaign ended, Billy received more invitations.

*God, if You're calling me to this full-time, then I had better understand what You want to tell Your people!* Billy studied Bible passages from Acts and Jeremiah, Colossians and Leviticus; he often spent entire nights taking notes, praying, listening. He devoured sermons from Moody and other spiritual giants that he admired, as well as Christian books and pamphlets. Billy began to frame his own thoughts in notebooks, adding scriptures, stories, and quotations. As he preached and studied, Billy grew in confidence. Hundreds in town halls, opera houses, and churches across the Midwest arrived early so they could find a seat to hear the earnest, entertaining young evangelist.

For the next twenty-five years, gaps in his speaking calendar would occur only when he needed a rest.

Throughout his life, Billy had never lacked a sense of humor. Now his homegrown wit stung and tickled listeners from Alton, Illinois, to Salida, Colorado.

"In every community are some folks the devil can catch with a bare hook."[3]

"You never hear of a man marrying a woman to reform her."[4]

"Find God and other folks will look a good deal better to you when you look at them through salvation. You will find your neighbor's house will look a good deal better if you only wash your own windows, old man."[5]

"Now, don't blame your parents, my friends. If you lived in a palace with a black heart, you would turn it into a slum. You turn a polecat loose in a parlor and you know which will change first, the parlor or the polecat."[6]

"You say, 'I had a bad start in life.' I am sorry. You say, 'I was born with the devil in me.' All right, you can be born again with the devil out of you in two minutes if you want to be."[7]

"No photographer could make a living taking pictures if he made them look just like you."[8]

Billy loved the churches that assisted in his crusades, but he often criticized them. "I want to explode the idea that love is blind. I tell you, love has an eagle's eyes."[9] He refused to take pity on pastors or church members: "The preacher who can't make his preaching interesting has no business in the pulpit. If he can't talk over ten minutes without making people begin to snap their watches and go to yawning all over the house, he has misunderstood the Lord about his call to preach."[10]

"I sometimes doubt whether the church needs new members one-half as much as she needs the old bunch made over."[11] Billy once told of a funeral where the minister did not show up. Determined that the man should not be buried without a few pious words, the grave digger decided to do the honor: "Dear friends, this corpse has been a member of this church for forty years!"[12]

Billy traveled to one prairie town after another to warn the people against procrastinating over their spiritual state. "Tonight when the last song is sung, the last prayer has been said, and we have all passed out into the night, and the lights have been switched off, and the place is dark, your chance, sinner, will be gone! If your heart is not soft before then, it is hardly likely that it will ever be so nearly won again. You say in your heart, 'Tomorrow!' but at daylight the doctor's buggy may be standing at your gate, the family may be grouped around your bed, with handkerchiefs at their eyes. The doctor, turning to them, may say, 'He is gone.' The undertaker may come and do his work. The friends may come and listen to such kind words as may be spoken of you, and then, as Mr. Moody once said of a man who died in spite of his prayers, they may take you, a Christless corpse, in a Christless coffin, and lay you in a Christless grave! O friends! If the Lord would draw back the veil which is between some of you and your coffin, you would leap back in horror, to find it so near that you could reach out and touch it. But you say, 'Tomorrow!' "[13]

*Lord, everywhere I go, I want to tell people about Jesus. I want them to know the one who gave up living in heaven to die for them. Help me to make it plain, Lord.*

"Nowhere do you find Him seeking the multitude, but He never avoided the individual," Billy told his congregations. "And His teaching was always adapted to the comprehension of those whom He taught. It is said that the common people heard Him gladly, and this shows that they understood what He said. He put the cookies on the lower shelf. No man had to take a dictionary with him when he went to hear the Sermon on the Mount."[14]

*Help me, Lord. Please help me always to put the cookies on the lower shelf for Your people.*

# TWELVE

Billy wrote Nell many homesick letters as he traveled from small town to small town. She answered with detailed accounts of Helen's learning to read and George's newest escapade. Sometimes both Billy and Nell wished he had "hung around" a little longer than the few days he had spent at Christmas. They planned many quick visits together when Billy spoke in northern Illinois, Michigan, or Indiana. Sometimes Nell would leave the children with her mother-in-law or her parents and join Billy in meetings in the Midwest.

Occasionally Jennie Sunday Stowell would attend the revivals, her face glowing with pride as she watched her son preach the gospel.

*Who would have thought it, Lord? Billy, a preacher!*

Billy Sunday scheduled more and more revivals as his fame grew.

He soon learned, however, that doing God's work in evangelism, as in baseball, did not guarantee things would go smoothly. In one midwestern town, Billy preached for two weeks, collected 127 conversion cards from new believers, and netted a total of thirty-three dollars.

Billy also had to manage all the church contacts, financial arrangements, precrusade publicity, and recruitment of choir, ushers, and other local workers by himself for several years.

*Sometimes, Lord, it's hard to concentrate on preaching Your Word when I have to figure out in every town where to find benches for people to sit on!*

Fortunately, his years with Chapman had taught Billy how to manage the endless details of an on-the-road ministry.

Because the churches and opera houses often could not contain the crowds of people who came to hear Billy, he purchased a large tent. When high winds rose on the prairies, he left his bed to spend half the night sitting on the guy ropes or checking the supports, praying his investment would not arrive in heaven before he did.

Often Billy's sensational reputation preceded him. Local religious leaders, having heard of his unorthodox antics, blunt rhetoric, and critical remarks about pastors, regarded him with suspicion. Saloon owners occasionally tried to block his arrival in their towns because a Billy Sunday crusade usually meant an immediate drop in profits. A newspaper in Elliott, Iowa, mentioned that the daily "northbound train brought thirty-five cases of liquor to Elliott, but the southbound train carried the stuff all back again."[1]

Billy's ministry prospered, and hundreds of rural Americans saw their communities profoundly affected by "the world's spiritual Tom Sawyer."[2] Journalists in Malvern, Iowa, had discussed the townspeople's skepticism as they anticipated Sunday's revival there. Billy's last meeting in Malvern saw more than a thousand worshipers attending his service.

People of all ages packed the Presbyterian Church to capacity every night, reported an incredulous journalist in Tecumseh, Nebraska. The congregation filled the pews. More worshipers crowded into chairs placed in the aisles. They even stood along the walls. Many in the town also attended Billy's afternoon meetings.

By 1900, Billy could afford to pay a full-time music director. He chose Fred Fisher, a former iron molder whom Billy had met through his friend Peter Bilhorn. A dedicated man, Fred had led revival choirs for several years, earning only four dollars a week. When Fred led the singing at an earlier meeting in Bedford, Iowa, directing enthusiastically as he always did, he almost tore off the sleeve of his ragged black suit coat.

*There is no reason why the Lord's servant should dress like this.* Billy took Fred to a local shop where the young man gasped at the luxury of fine, warm cloth and trousers that reached all the way down to his shiny, new shoes.

Billy used his tent more and more, but he hesitated to take it to Salida, Colorado, in September. Local citizens declared the weather usually remained temperate until middle October, so, as usual, he set it up the day before the revival was to begin. The meetings went exceptionally well; Billy enjoyed the free-and-easy atmosphere of the West and the openness of its people. The night before his last meeting, he went to bed early, anticipating the exciting last day of the campaign. Billy always considered the final service the pinnacle of his crusades, but he also knew he would soon wave good-bye to people he had learned to love, watching them crowd the train station, waving handkerchiefs, and singing "Blest Be the Tie That Binds" as his train slowly puffed down the tracks. He needed a good night's sleep to handle all of that.

Billy awoke shivering the next morning. Had the temperature dropped that much? He stumbled around the room, searching for his trunk. Where was the long underwear Nell had packed? He peered out his hotel window. Snow! Three to four feet of snow engulfed all of Salida!

"Lord! Why have You sent the winter version of the Flood? And especially on the last day of the crusade?" Billy held his head in his hands. The streets were nearly impassable, even if the tent were intact. Surely the inhabitants of Salida would do the sane thing tonight: stay home by their warm fires!

"If they do, Lord, I don't know what I'll do!" Not only did the last service symbolize the climax of the crusade, but Billy had made a practice of accepting only the last night's freewill offering as payment for his services.

He had, as usual, assured the church community of Salida that he would require no other salary.

"Oh, God. The rent is due back home. We'll soon have to buy coal for the winter, and the children need shoes and warm coats. Nell does her best, Lord, but we can't afford to lose this offering. We just can't!"

"Reverend Sunday?" A friendly fist pounded his door. "Don't you worry none. We're fixin' to do some snowplowing out here in front of the hotel, then we'll go take a look at the tent."

Billy almost groaned. "I'll be down in a second," he answered, yanking on his clothes.

When he went out into the street, Billy's spirits rose. As far as he could see, men and boys and their horses were breaking paths through drifts on the streets of Salida.

"Snow usually comes a little later," said Clement Howard, the Presbyterian church member who had knocked on Billy's door. "But we're used to a bit of weather around here. We'll fix it up d'rectly, and folks'll be able to come by sleigh to the meetin' tonight." He spoke to his adult sons, then gestured with his head. "The boys'll keep at it whilst we walk a piece to look at your tent."

All of Billy's earlier optimism fell as they approached the ruined tent, covered with heavy snow. Even if they managed to remove the snow, Billy knew the weight had damaged the framework extensively and the raging blizzard winds the night before had shredded the canvas.

*Lord, I feel as flat as this tent.*

"Don't b'lieve the tent's goin' to be much good tonight," said Clem, "but folks'll gather at the opry house. You'll see, Reverend."

Billy trudged back to the hotel and borrowed a shovel, grimly attacking the snow on the wooden sidewalks as if it were his mortal enemy. He worked for hours, viciously throwing shovelful after shovelful of the evil stuff out of the way.

"Don't go wearin' yourself down, Rev. Sunday," drawled Clem. "You got to preach tonight." He flicked the reins on his horses' backs and headed home to change and eat before the service.

Billy wearily set the shovel by the front door and went inside to eat Mrs. Gray's delicious chicken and noodles.

*If the Lord wants me to speak tonight,* he mused, *He's going to have to supply the power to do it.*

"Good-bye," Billy called to the men, women, and children who had gathered to see him off. "The Lord bless you all!"

The crowd answered with cheers, tears, and smiles. The warm sun had already melted some of the snow, so many had gathered to wish Billy well as he boarded his train. A soprano who had persistently sung off-key began a hymn. *Is there one in every town?* Billy wondered. Others quickly joined her—*Probably to drown her out*, Billy thought. But the earnest, loving faces moved Billy, and he sat motionless for some time as the train gathered speed.

*Lord, You worked it all out. Those who could came to the opera house. You helped me preach, and lost souls found You.* Billy thanked God for the hard labor that had made the last service possible.

*Not many in Salida are rich, but like the widow woman You saw in the temple, they gave all they had.* The offering Billy had hidden in his valise was not large, but it would pay for the Sundays' rent and coal and winter clothes.

*Lord, You are faithful, even when I am not. But I think You're telling me to use tabernacles from now on, not tents.*

Billy had first conceived of tabernacles to house his revival crowds in 1901. Workers constructed a circular, wide building in Perry, Iowa. It was built of full-length pine lumber that could be recycled for other use. Its sides could be easily removed to create large exits in case of a fire or other emergencies. When Billy spoke from the pulpit on the five-foot-high platform in the center of the building, he could be heard in almost every corner of the room, an innovation in the days before microphones. Local businessmen and clergy built the Perry tabernacle at a cost of seven hundred dollars. It housed one thousand worshipers, but the crowds soon outgrew the first Billy Sunday tabernacle.

Workers also smoothed pine shavings and sawdust on the floors to minimize audience noise. Newspapers in the Northwest soon alluded to new converts walking down the aisles as "hitting the sawdust trail," referring to an actual practice by loggers who scattered sawdust in order to find their way home through the immense forests of the area.

As Billy's crusades increased in number and attendance, so did the size of his tabernacles. Construction workers grew so experienced at building them according to the Perry blueprint that they could estimate accurately how far Billy's voice would carry. But even when the New York City tabernacle was designed to seat twenty thousand, throngs of eager people came early only to find the mammoth tabernacle overflowing. They usually waited patiently outside until a later service began.

"Nell, this is almost like heaven."

Billy and Nell sat on the back porch of their summer cottage, "Illinois," in the quiet twilight of Winona Lake, Indiana, 1903. They had discovered the pleasant little town when Billy first spoke at the Winona Lake Conference Center. The center, a midwestern Chautauqua-like headquarters, held Bible studies, prayer meetings, lectures, and seminars for pastors, as well as Sunday school and church workers, throughout the summer. Funded primarily by industrialists such as John M. Studebaker and H. J. Heinz, the organization provided not only Christian education for adults, teens, and children, but also wholesome entertainment and fun activities for its participants.

Billy, exhausted from his strenuous crusade schedule, especially disliked the oppressive heat, dirt, and noise of Chicago during the summer. He gratefully accepted invitations from his old friend and employer Dr.

J. W. Chapman, who now headed the conference center. Billy and Nell tried to set aside extended time with their children in Winona Lake each summer. Both the Sundays felt the wholesome, small-town atmosphere benefitted their family; they dreamed of building a permanent home there someday.

Now they listened to the tranquil night noises and watched the stars come out in the velvety blue-black sky. A two-month stretch of nonstop meetings would greet Billy in August, but for several weeks Billy intended to spend as much time with Nell and the children as possible.

"I'm glad you're not preaching till Sunday services, Billy."

He chuckled. "It was hard to turn Dr. Chapman down this time, but I knew it would all start again if I agreed to preach at the conference center during the week."

"Don't forget you promised to take the older children swimming tomorrow," Nell reminded him. George and Helen loved romping with their athletic father on the beach. He would turn endless somersaults, walk on his hands, and throw them, squealing with delight, into the clear, shallow water.

"George wants to fish," said Billy. "Sounds good to me, too. We'll go out tomorrow evening and catch a mess of bluegills."

"He does so much better when you're with us, Billy." She grimaced a little at the thought of her lovable but conniving son. At ten years of age, George usually managed to get his own way.

"Wish I could have you and the children with me all the time, Nell."

The Sundays all struggled with Billy's long absences.

Billy Jr., who was born in 1901, was ten days old before his father returned from a crusade meeting in Harlan, Iowa. Now a toddler, he often maintained a distance from Billy Sr., until his father cajoled and tickled him into sitting on his lap.

Once when Billy was about to depart again for a crusade, Helen begged him to stay with her. "Papa, you're the best friend I've got, and I don't want you to go away. Let's go to bed and tell stories."[3] Billy promised the child presents when he returned. When she requested a new dress and a ring, he searched for the prettiest gifts he could find: a lovely ring with a small turquoise stone and a new blue striped silk dress. Helen, however, had changed her mind. "Papa, I don't want a ring. I don't want a dress. I just want you. You're the best friend I've got. Stay at home with me, Papa, and I won't never want anything but you!"[4]

Nell, too, grappled with everyday pressures and loneliness, but she had long ago decided to endure Billy's absences as part of his calling as an evangelist. *God's work comes first.*

Now as the summer moon smiled down on the two of them and stroked the waves of Winona Lake, Nell put negative thoughts out of her head.

*I want to enjoy our time together while we have it,* she resolved. Nell held Billy's hand. The two savored the silence that spoke more than pages of words.

*Thank You, Lord, for Nell,* thought Billy. *If only all other married people had what we have together.*

An eminent Chicago presbytery questioned Billy as he sought ordination in 1903. The examining board had to admit that he displayed occasional ignorance on the fine points of church history. One committee member spoke for them all, however, when he declared that Billy should receive ordination without question: "Mr. Sunday certainly knows basic scriptural doctrine. And he has led more people to Christ than all of us if we added our converts together!" The examination ended abruptly, and the Presbyterian Church officially declared his ordination valid.

Billy seemed determined to confirm their findings. People waited outside his tabernacles for hours, then crammed benches and standing areas inside. They often listened to two-hour sermons given in clear, sometimes very harsh, language. Billy did not tolerate Satan, that "cloven-hoofed, forked-tailed, blazing-eyed Old Devil,"[5] or his followers: "Some men are so rotten and vile that they ought to be disinfected and made to take a bath in carbolic acid and formaldehyde."[6] When praying for those especially engulfed in sin, Billy advised the Lord to don rubber gloves when He handled them. He condemned breaking the Ten Commandments and what he considered the worst of sins: drinking, immorality, family abuse, and gambling. But Billy went on to enumerate more specific offenses. He loathed popular dances: "their can-can and other licentious, wriggling squirming dances that in our day we call the turkey trot and the grizzly bear and other God-forsaken hell-born dances."[7] "You stand there and watch. . .your wife folded in his long, voluptuous, sensual embrace, their bodies swaying one against the other, their limbs twining and entwining, her head resting on his breast, they breathe the vitiated air beneath the glittering candelabra, and the spell of the music, and you stand there and tell me that there is no harm in it!"[8] He also deplored card playing, billiard playing, even children playing marbles (for keeps) and jacks instead of dolls for girls. He saw women's obsession with pets (particularly small house dogs) as decadent. Smoking, gossiping, indulging in vulgar humor and trashy novels, listening to suggestive music, wasting money, theatergoing, and using bad language also made his "sin list," as well as birth control, laziness, avarice, lewdness, and the use of makeup.

Billy also had no patience with lukewarm religiosity: "Lord, save us from off-handed, flabby-cheeked, brittle-boned, weak-kneed, thin-skinned, pliable, plastic, spineless, effeminate, ossified three-karat Christianity."[9]

Despite the severity of his messages, people swarmed to his meetings. Some likened Billy to John the Baptist for his personal courage and eccentricity, as well as his ever-present call for repentance. "He uses the word 'hell' so freely and frequently that it seems like a pet in the household of his vocabulary. And yet the people nearly fall over one another in the rush and crush to hear him. . . ."[10]

Billy's rural crowds, composed mostly of respectable, hardworking citizens, appeared to understand he wanted to protect them from the infecting powers of seemingly harmless practices. "When I preach to you of God, I'm not your enemy; I'm the enemy of the devil who is dragging you down to hell. I ask no quarter of the devil," declared Billy, "and I give none."[11] So Billy thundered and raged as he preached. He joked and laughed; turned flips and skidded into imaginary home plates; shadowboxed the devil while standing on a stool; performed one-man skits, voicing the lines of eight or nine characters; even smashed a chair or two—anything to make his point and bring his listeners closer to God and farther away from sin.

"I know men," Billy told one congregation. "I know their trials, their temptations, and I know there are men in hell tonight who never meant to be there any more than you do."[12] He leaped for joy when he shook the hands of the people who jammed the aisles at his invitation, much as he had once jumped as he captured impossible fly balls for the White Stockings and the Alleghenies.

*That's one more on Your side, Lord,* Billy thought as he spoke with each new convert. *And that's one less on the devil's team.*

# THIRTEEN

Towns and cities across the United States welcomed Billy. He preached to ever-increasing audiences who pondered the evangelist's words and changed their lifestyles in response to his tough, tender message of repentance and new life in Christ.

In Wilkes-Barre, Pennsylvania, a store clerk who had stolen $5.35 ten years before returned the money to his astonished employer. More than ten thousand people in the town, most of them men, marched in a law-and-order parade, demonstrating their support for laws that closed saloons on Sundays.

A Decatur, Illinois, newspaper recorded that businesses, lodge meetings, and even baseball games were canceled so the town might focus its attention on the revival meetings of Billy Sunday. One reporter, while buying a shirt, tried to provoke a shopkeeper into a negative reaction toward the evangelist and was promptly shown the door.

Saloon keepers in South Bend and Mishawaka, Indiana, figured their intake lessened by 40 percent. Businessmen saw long-outstanding debts paid; even anonymous payments for shoplifted merchandise arrived daily in the mail. One store owner in Elwood, Indiana, received two dollars for a knife pilfered two years before.

In Fargo, North Dakota, the city government passed laws that severely restricted its brothel business; within a year, police had closed more than seventy houses of prostitution, nearly eliminating the city's red-light district.

Many noted that Christians in the communities where Billy preached renounced their mediocrity. Tearing down denominational barriers, they gladly reached out to each other, the new converts, and the communities in which they lived.

"God is doing wonderful things all over America," Billy marveled.

"I can't keep up with all these requests for crusades," laughed Nell, who helped schedule his meetings from their home in Chicago. "Too bad you can't be in ten places at one time!"

"If I could, one of me would always be with you and the children, Nell." He took her hand. "Helen is at Valparaiso University now, and George is going to prep school this year. I know Billy Jr., and Paul are still young, but do you think that you could travel with me more, Nell? I miss you so much when we're apart."

Nell touched his cheek. Although small wrinkles clustered at the corners of his eyes, Billy still resembled the lovesick young baseball player who had pursued her years before. "Your mother would help. And perhaps Nora Lynn would live here full-time." Jennie Sunday

Stowell, newly widowed, might enjoy some extended time with the boys, Nell thought, and Nora, a sensible, pleasant woman, had assisted Nell with the housekeeping since Paul's birth in 1907. "We could think about it."

Better than anyone, Nell knew Billy's strengths and weaknesses. His burgeoning evangelistic career drained him emotionally, so he struggled with the endless details that needed attention at every crusade. Nell had helped him all she could while remaining at home, but more and more, she realized that Billy would never achieve his best without her at his side.

Nell squeezed his hand. "Let's pray about it together, Billy."

During the next busy years of his ministry, Billy often thanked God for Nell's management of his crusades. From 1896 to 1906, Billy had spent the great majority of his time in towns that numbered under ten thousand in population.[1] But as his reputation spread across the United States, he found himself speaking in larger cities. In 1909, he conducted his first crusade in a city with a population of more than one hundred thousand people: Spokane, Washington.[2] From that point on, his ministry increasingly focused on urban centers, and the size and complexity of his crusade meetings grew with the cities' populations.

*If Nell had not been here to run things, how could I have ever concentrated on preaching the gospel?* Billy shook his head in wonder at Nell's gift for organization.

"Ma" Sunday had become the unchallenged authority in all practical matters pertaining to Billy's crusades. "Evangelism à la Billy Sunday was approached like a business with Billy the chairman of the board, and Nell as the chief executive officer."[3] She planned, commanded, enforced, hired, fired, and publicized. Billy considered himself blessed with talented assistants such as Homer Rodeheaver, his music leader. But Nell's word always superceded other opinions. Under her leadership, Billy's crusades functioned like a well-rehearsed symphony orchestra, with each section playing its part. Nell also possessed a gift for understanding the people who tried to gain access to her husband. If less-than-sympathetic journalists came to his doorstep, she was there to smilingly head them off at the pass. If businessmen approached Billy, she somehow knew which ones would build his ministry and which would damage it. Few people cared to cross Ma Sunday. Once, when irreverent young men attired in wigs, bustles, and high heels attempted to "crash" a ladies-only prayer meeting, a grim Nell escorted them sternly to the door and slammed it behind them.

Nell also saw that her husband ate and slept properly. Billy often became irritable and tense as crusades approached; Nell's calm efficiency and diplomacy insulated him from pressures that might have caused his temper to erupt like a volcano. She also protected him after crusades, permitting him to convalesce from his campaigns as if from an illness. Although Billy shook thousands of hands and talked with hundreds during his meetings, he needed solitude in which to study and practice his messages. Nell, his personal guardian angel, made sure that no one interrupted Billy's quiet times.

She tried to keep the home fires burning in the midst of the Sundays' chaotic schedules. They built a permanent residence in Winona Lake in 1911, an Arts and Crafts–style brown bungalow on a hill, christening it "Mt. Hood." The Arts and Crafts architectural movement emphasized simplicity in living and closeness to nature; the Sundays had reflected this philosophy in their home, hoping "Mt. Hood" would provide a peaceful haven for their family away from the stress of the crusades. Nell had designed the layout of the house herself, including a large parlor and dining room with many windows and sleeping porches at either end of the house to catch the fresh evening breezes off the lake. A long hallway in the center of the house displayed her own oil paintings and a growing collection of autographed pictures of famous friends, including several presidents. She had given in to the little boys' demand for a bright red bedroom, and had her kitchen painted leaf green. Although most homemakers of the era considered their kitchens purely functional, painting them a sterile, bare white, Nell loved color and further decorated hers with fine china teapots and vases. She missed "Mt. Hood," with the Ansonian clock on the fireplace mantel, the olive velveteen loveseat she had shared with Billy since their courting days, the brilliant tapestry of the family macaw that she had worked herself and hung in the dining room.

*I even miss the noise when that silly bird and Prince and the boys all get into it.* Nell shook her head, smiling ruefully. When she closed her eyes, she could see Billy Jr., fearlessly riding his velocipede in front of "Mt. Hood." She could feel the silky-softness of Paul's blond hair and see the dimples in his hands as he petted their Airedale terrier. Even though Helen and George were so much older, Nell also missed them deeply.

She communicated regularly with her invaluable housekeeper, Nora Lynn, who remained with them until all the Sunday children became adults. She and Billy wrote loving letters to a homesick Helen at college, encouragement and warnings to a gifted but mischievous George at boarding school, and affectionate notes to Billy Jr., and little Paul at home. Sometimes Nell arranged surprise meetings on birthdays or holidays. She often thanked God for the telephone and the telegraph. She tried to schedule blocks of time within the year when the family could spend uninterrupted time together. Nell kept an emergency bag packed, whether at home or on the road, so that she could hop a train with a few minutes' notice, whether the women's crusade prayer meetings in Charleston required her special touch or a sick child in Winona Lake needed her at his bedside. Ma Sunday, friends realized later, traveled twice as many miles as her husband.

The crusade staff adored the volatile, charismatic Billy. They appreciated Nell's intelligence and industry, but did not always like her, since she spoke her mind freely and expected them to do exactly as she said.

Together, Billy and Nell built a crusade organization that became a model for future American revivalists. As Billy's fame grew, gifted men and women joined him to provide the framework for his meetings.

Homer Rodeheaver, a former coal miner from Tennessee, not only functioned as choir director but served as Billy's master of ceremonies from 1909 until 1929. The tall, clean-cut man in the white suit had a knack for drawing the crowd in and warming them up. His homey southern accent and suave voice balanced Billy's fiery sermons and impassioned altar calls. "Rody" even captivated the children in the audiences, sometimes playing magician or doing hand-puppet skits. A member of a military band during the Spanish-American War, he played his trombone superbly. He acted as if the trombone were part of him, sticking it under his arm, directing with it, spinning and playing it. Eventually Rody started his own recording studio and sold more than one million copies of his recording of "The Old Rugged Cross," as well as thousands of copies of the crusade hymnbook, *Songs for Service.*

Audiences loved Rody's rich baritone voice, too, when he occasionally sang solos or in duets. But his choirs became a trademark of Billy Sunday revivals—choirs composed of thousands of voices, fervently singing a wide variety of hymns from "A Mighty Fortress Is Our God" to the more contemporary music of Charles Gabriel and B. D. Ackley. When a multitude triumphantly echoed "Stand Up, Stand Up for Jesus" and "Onward, Christian Soldiers" throughout Billy Sunday's tabernacles, distracted audiences quieted in awe. The crusade goers then joined the choir, singing "If Your Heart Keeps Right," "In the Garden," "Beyond the Sunset," and "Tell Me the Story of Jesus." When Rody raised his arms to pull powerful, roof-raising music from the congregation, only to soften it suddenly to a reverent whisper, even nonmusical participants felt themselves part of an angelic choir.

Other music assistants helped Rody create a musical program unmatched by any other. George Brewster, who had sung and acted in New York theaters, served as Billy's main soloist. Bob Matthews became his "secretary/pianist" and helped with organization and publicity, along with his musical duties.

Billy also employed advance men who visited his crusade sites weeks ahead of time, speaking to pastors, lay leaders, and their churches, recruiting and organizing workers for the upcoming campaign. All were excellent speakers, from his first advance man, Fred Siebert, the

"Cowboy Evangelist," whom he hired in 1905, to James E. Walker and Billy's own son George, who spearheaded later crusades. They accomplished herculean tasks in relatively short times. A crusade council was informed eight months before the 1915 Boston campaign that close to twenty thousand volunteers would be required: two thousand ushers; seven hundred office workers; two hundred door attendants; five thousand prayer meeting leaders; one thousand women to solicit support from local businessmen; one thousand women to evangelize female employees in factories, hospitals, and hotels; five hundred child-care volunteers; and eight thousand choir members. Advance men, working with the area pastors, inspired more than thirty-five thousand Bostonians to volunteer.[4]

Since Billy esteemed his wife's abilities so highly, it was no surprise that he included other women on his leadership team. Grace Saxe set up Bible classes in area schools and churches, along with Frances Miller.

Mrs. William Asher, who directed women's activities, organized volunteers to initiate Bible studies and prayer meetings in offices, factories, YWCAs, and area stores. She contacted doctors' wives and nurses in order to reach women in hospitals and used teen girls and college coeds to lead groups in churches. Annie MacLaren, a Scottish-born singer previously employed by Moody Institute, headed the program for children.

Dr. Isaac Ward directed the men's groups. He set up meetings among railroad and factory workers, in stores and prisons and trolley barns. Dr. Ward usually brought a Salvation Army trumpet soloist with him to play "Brighten the Corner" or "Since Jesus Came Into My Heart" wherever he went. Surprisingly, the hardened men in those rough places usually sang along.

Billy even had his own postmaster, Fred Buse, who managed the voluminous crusade correspondence, sometimes handling as much mail as a small-town post office. He made sure that communication between Billy, his assistants, and area church leaders flowed efficiently. He also distributed convert cards, based on their addresses, to the appropriate churches. Fred sometimes had to sort and issue thousands of cards after only one meeting.

Billy's publicity team often produced better results than those of major businesses. They made sure area newspapers were well supplied with crusade information, captivating (and usually unorthodox) photos of the evangelist, and copies of his sermons. They regularly contacted magazines and other publications that might be interested in his story. Billy Sunday souvenirs were always available for purchase at his crusades: hymnbooks, posters, biographies, and pamphlets.

Billy loved to participate in the endless promotional events his team staged: ball games played by teams composed of area merchants; a wagon ride with the oldest citizen in the county; photo sessions with famous government officials, industrialists, or high-society leaders; and Sunday school parades that sometimes numbered in the thousands. Despite his dislike of the entertainment business, he welcomed a group of Al Jolson's Winter Garden troupe of showgirls to the platform during his Boston crusade. Later in his career, he would befriend movie director Cecil B. De Mille; photographers would catch him "hamming it up" with actors such as Douglas Fairbanks. Once he even hired a "giant," a former employee of Barnum and Bailey's circus, to usher at some of his crusades.

But the real attraction for congregations across the United States was, of course, Billy Sunday himself. Each night the athletic, boyish evangelist wore a perfect, wrinkleless suit, his patent leather shoes reflecting the bright kerosene lights, his trendy tie held by a diamond stickpin. He darted across the platform, whirled, hopped, dove, flopped, and slid until he seemed only a blur. Occasionally Billy thumped or even mounted his pulpit to shake his fist and make his point. Sometimes he caressed his audience with his words. One listener said that "Sunday could talk about a rail fence and make you see more beauty in its vineclad nooks and corners than another could show you in a cathedral."[5]

At other times he spoke so bluntly about sex, hell, and damnation that he was accused of vulgarity and blasphemy. "Paul said he would rather speak five words that were understood than ten thousand in an unknown tongue, and that hits me," retorted Billy. "I want people to know what I mean, and that is why I try to get down to where they live. What do I care if some juff-eyed dainty little dibbly-dibbly goes tibbly-tibbly around because I use plain Anglo-Saxon words?"[6] Billy thundered and whispered, roared and joked until more sedate clergy demanded that he "smooth down" his abrasive style.

"If I did that," Billy answered his critics, "I wouldn't have any more people to preach to than you men do."[7]

From his early ministry in Chicago's slums, Billy had targeted alcohol as a major cause of the suffering of humanity. His primary goal was to save souls—no one who attended a Billy Sunday crusade could doubt it—but Billy also fought against alcohol consumption advocates and suppliers with every ounce of energy he possessed.

In his famous "Booze Sermon" (actually entitled "Get on the Water Wagon"), Billy declared that "the saloon is the sum of all villainies. It is worse than war or pestilence. It is the crime of crimes. It is the parent of crimes and the mother of sins. . . . And to license such an incarnate fiend of hell is the dirtiest, most low down, damnable business on top of this old earth.

"The saloons fill the jails and the penitentiaries, the poorhouses and insane asylums. Who has to pay the bills? The landlord who doesn't get the rent, because the money goes for whiskey, the butcher and the grocer and the charitable person who takes pity on the children of drunkards, and the taxpayer who supports the insane asylums and other institutions that the whiskey business fills with human wrecks.

"Do away with the accursed business, and you will not have to put up to support them. . . .

"You say, 'People will drink it anyway.' Not by my vote. 'They will steal anyway.' Not by my vote. You are the sovereign people, and what are *you* going to do about it?"[8]

He raked the consciences of his audiences. "The saloon will take off the shirt from the back of a shivering man. It will take the coffin from under the dead. It will take the milk from the breast of the poor mother who is the wife of a drinking man. It will take the crust of bread from the hand of the hungry child. It cares for nothing but itself—for its dirty profits. It will keep your boy out of college. It will make your daughter a prostitute. It will bury your wife in the potter's field. It will send you to hell."[9]

Billy's audiences often answered his challenge with determined, nitty-gritty action. Thousands at his crusades sang "De Brewer's Big Horses Can't Run Over Me" and "John Barleycorn's Body Lies a Mouldering in the Clay" with Klaxon horns, automobile whistles, and bells echoing raucously in the background. They signed petitions and pledges, marched in temperance parades, and joined organizations such as the Anti-Saloon League and the Women's Christian Temperance Union. A converted sheriff in Wilkes-Barre, Pennsylvania, ruthlessly opposed the saloons under his jurisdiction, promoting antialcohol laws to the fullest extent. The Burlington, Iowa, mayor closed the saloons in his town on Sunday.

Brewery and bar owners viewed the rising antialcohol tide with alarm. Some joined forces to combat the threat to their livelihood, as two hundred liquor merchants and saloon keepers in Pittsburgh did before Billy came to town in 1913. They discussed their concerns with sympathetic local politicians who promised to stand for "personal liberty." To the dismay of their proalcohol constituents, some of the lobbyists were converted in the crusade and told journalists they planned to support the temperance movement thereafter.

Increasing numbers of towns in the Midwest went "dry." A Decatur, Illinois, saloon displayed this sign after Billy's six-week crusade in that city: "Closed Until Further Notice by Order of Billy Sunday."[10] Mason City, Iowa, and Steubenville, Ohio, followed suit. Billy and his staff began to visualize whole states going dry.

When businessmen and pastors in Wheeling, West Virginia, and Spokane, Washington, chartered special trains to crisscross their states and invited Billy to speak in favor of prohibition at each stop, he eagerly agreed. Near-rabid audiences cheered Billy's "Booze Sermon" wildly; some waved white handkerchiefs. Reporters rode the train with Billy, writing column after column about the incredible persuasive powers of the evangelist and the huge crowds he attracted.

"Wouldn't it be wonderful if the whole country got rid of that accursed stuff?" Billy could visualize it, just as he visualized the conversion of thousands. "God will make it happen. I know He will!" he shouted to the applauding spectators.

In December 1914, more than a thousand determined people paraded down Pennsylvania Avenue to the Capitol in the bitter Washington, D.C., winter weather. They bore a resolution that forbade the creation and sale of alcohol in the United States. Congressman Richard P. Hobson of Alabama, a fervent temperance advocate, gladly presented the proposal to the House of Representatives. After months of debate and increasing pressure from prohibition advocates, the House voted in favor of the resolution but failed to reach the two-thirds majority that would have sent a constitutional amendment to the states for consideration. Undaunted by the temporary setback, prohibition forces resolved to double their efforts. Victory was in the air!

Their cause gained momentum when two prohibition champions joined forces. Billy had long admired William Jennings Bryan, a fiery Christian orator and former presidential candidate who for years had held his audiences spellbound. Sunday loaned Bryan his choir and tabernacle in Philadelphia for a rally there, and the old warrior filled it with thousands of reform-minded listeners who readily signed abstinence pledges.

Nearby, in Trenton, New Jersey, Billy held both houses of the New Jersey legislature spellbound with his impassioned plea for prohibition. Although it was the first time a clergyman had ever addressed them in their assembly chamber, Billy did not change his message or his methods; at one point, he scaled the desk of the Speaker of the House. Startled lawmakers and spectators in the packed galleries, after the initial shock, began to cheer and applaud. At the end of the unorthodox "service," the politicians presented Billy with a large horseshoe of red and white flowers that enclosed the state seal of New Jersey.

Business groups and industrialists around the country also pushed for prohibition, believing their employees would produce more effectively if they led sober lifestyles.

By 1916, 51 percent of Americans resided in areas where alcohol was prohibited.[11] The prohibition movement continued to sweep the country as more and more areas went dry.

But not all United States citizens supported the idea of alcohol abstinence. Many immigrant groups that regarded drinking alcohol as an everyday part of their cultures viewed prohibition forces with hostility. Prominent citizens such as attorney Clarence Darrow deplored what they regarded as the imminent loss of their personal liberty. Magazines such as the *Liberal Advocate* and the *Iconoclast* blasted prohibition and its proponents—especially Billy Sunday—as reactionary. The liquor industry tried to discredit Billy as a raving fanatic.

Billy responded by holding a crusade in Detroit, Michigan, in 1916. Personal-liberty advocates and prohibition supporters alike agreed that Michigan would play a key role in the country's stance on alcohol. Soon the voters in that state would decide whether they wanted Michigan dry or wet.

Billy built his largest tabernacle yet and mesmerized sixteen thousand people at each meeting, praying, leaping, whirling, performing the acrobatic feats that glued his audience to him. At one Detroit rally, he welcomed an unprecedented twenty-nine thousand raucous blue-collar workers. Many identified their trades with colorful homemade banners; others responded with deafening yells when Rody recognized each factory or workplace. The astute master of ceremonies had designed the congregational singing, as he often did, around some of the congregation's occupations (he had once led "Wash Me as White as Snow" in honor of a large group of launderers). When Billy preached his uncompromising "Booze Sermon," the men cheered him like a hero, despite the fact that many of them regularly drank a beer in a neighborhood tavern after work each day. Hundreds walked down the sawdust-strewn aisles to ask Christ into their lives and to promise they would never again drink alcohol.

During the Detroit revival, Billy made special trips to Saginaw, Ypsilanti, and Ann Arbor, where he preached to a riotous audience of students from the University of Michigan. There he vowed he would never stop fighting those who permitted alcohol manufacture and consumption. "I will fight them till hell freezes over, then I'll buy a pair of skates and fight 'em on the ice."[12]

On his last day in Detroit, which attracted fifty thousand listeners, Billy predicted America would pass prohibition within eight to ten years.

Finally, he spent a day in Grand Rapids, pleading with his audience of seven thousand to vote for the banning of alcohol.

*Tomorrow's the day, Lord. Tomorrow Michigan decides if she'll follow You or follow the devil.* Late that night Billy dragged his weary body into the house where the crusade staff was staying. He flopped down on the comfortable bed in his room, only to stare at the ceiling for two hours. He rose as quietly as he could, but Nell's soft touch stopped him.

"Billy, you need your sleep. Tomorrow's a big day."

"Ma, I can't close my eyes. What good does it do just to lie here?"

"What good does it do to pace all night? At least you'll rest a little if you stay in bed." She rubbed his shoulders harder with her strong hands and felt his tense muscles unknot a little. "You did all you could, Billy."

"Did I, Nell? Did I?" He turned to face her. That question always tortured him at the end of every crusade.

"Yes, Billy, you did. Now it's up to God." Nell smoothed his still-plentiful hair and smiled. She pulled him down gently, and he cuddled close to her. Nell began to massage his shoulders once more.

Billy could not sleep the next night, either, but this time, he and his staff celebrated a stupendous victory. Michigan had gone dry!

"Impossible," Billy hooted. "They said it was impossible. Detroit would go wet by at least twenty-five thousand votes. That would make the difference. But the newspaper says the wets only took it by 1,368 votes. Thank You, Lord!" If Billy had not believed dancing was a sin, he would have danced all night long.

He and Nell headed for Winona Lake for a well-deserved rest. Soon, Billy knew, he would encounter more challenges, more criticism. Michigan was only the beginning. His enemies would attack him without mercy as a rigid fanatic who enjoyed stripping people of their choices.

*So let them come after me,* thought Billy. *Let them call me a fanatic or whatever they want to. I believe God will let me see the day when John Barleycorn is dead forever in the U.S.A.!*

# FOURTEEN

I don't want your money," Billy told the enormous crowd that packed the New York City tabernacle in 1917. He announced he would contribute all proceeds above the expenses of the massive crusade to the American Red Cross and the YMCA for their service to America's soldiers fighting in faraway Europe. When the roof-lifting shouts of approval finally died down, Billy held out his hands to the congregation: "I want you. I want to win your souls to Jesus."[1]

By contributing the unthinkable amount of $120,000 to those charities, Billy wanted to accomplish several goals.

First and foremost, he genuinely wanted the thousands of New Yorkers that filled the "Glory Barn" and waited outside for hours to know that Jesus Christ loved them and that Billy Sunday loved them. The value of their eternal souls far surpassed that of the dollars they dropped into his offering plates.

Secondly, he wanted to still the constant rumors

of his alleged greed. He had publicized the fact that the Chautauqua, filmmakers, and even circus owners had approached him with lucrative offers, and he had turned them all down to preach the gospel. During this New York crusade, Billy tried once more to define his attitude toward material wealth.

It was true, he affirmed, that the Sundays had purchased a ranch in Oregon and maintained their modest home in Winona Lake, Indiana.

"They keep saying we spent forty thousand dollars building this house! Didn't spend a penny over forty-eight hundred dollars to build *and* furnish it," insisted Billy.

He openly stated his wealth was a reward from God, but he and Nell managed their funds carefully, giving generously to others in need, as John D. Rockefeller Jr., found when he quietly investigated Billy's financial dealings before the crusade. Billy Sunday enjoyed providing plentifully for his family, but he wanted his opponents to realize he was not the multimillionaire they declared him to be.

Finally, Billy was glad to do what he could to help American soldiers in the war against the German Kaiser, whom he regarded as a near incarnation of Satan himself. "The Kaiser plays no favorites. He'd just as soon train his big guns upon an American woman with a baby at her breast as upon a Belgian cathedral, a Red Cross station, or a hospital; it's all the same to him."[2] Besides his main evangelistic theme of salvation through Jesus Christ, Billy emphasized patriotism in his New York City campaign. The choir and congregation sang "America" and "The Battle Hymn of the Republic" while Billy scaled his big oak pulpit and waved an American flag. He issued calls for enlistment and permitted the construction of six recruiting centers outside his tabernacle. Billy spoke frequently with groups of servicemen, urging them to serve God and country with all their hearts.

Even the ever-optimistic Billy Sunday couldn't have dreamed of the success of the New York crusade in 1917. From the beginning of his ministry, he had expected the aisles to fill with people who would repent and surrender their lives to Jesus Christ. He had seen hundreds converted in his earlier crusades in Burlington, Iowa, and Columbus, Ohio, then thousands in Philadelphia, Boston, and Chicago. He had even held a 1915 revival in New York in which five Yankee ballplayers, including Frank "Home Run" Baker, responded to Billy's direct warning about their eternal destiny in hell. During the 1917 ten-week revival in the sprawling, busy metropolis, a record-breaking one hundred thousand people signed conversion cards. When critics insisted that many of his so-called converts were upstanding church members, Billy admitted to that possibility.

*But Lord, sometimes the church members are the ones that need to repent the most.*

Billy and Nell spent a great deal of time with the "upper crust" in New York. He attended dinners with Rockefeller and General Leonard Wood. Governor Charles Whitman supported him openly. His friend Theodore Roosevelt wrote that he considered Billy the foremost reformer in the United States. But he also met with newspaper carriers and groups of high-school girls, as well as the derelicts at Hadley Rescue Hall in the Bowery, where he told the alcoholics, "joy ladies," and down-and-outers that God cared for them as much as He did those on Fifth Avenue.

As usual, Billy's crusade inspired not only religious

fervor, patriotism, and volunteerism, but plenty of criticism, as well. Some leading Christians declared that Billy not only borrowed from others' sermons, he plagiarized large portions of them. Intellectual clergymen deplored his coarse vaudeville style; labor activists accused him of close ties with prominent industrialists who exploited their workers; and two doctors warned that his approach was harmful to children. Famous newspaper artist Boardman Robinson, who had visited war-torn Europe, satirized Billy's passionate patriotism in his cartoons.

Isadora Duncan, a prominent dancer at the Metropolitan Opera House, told the press that she did not appreciate Billy's including her, as well as Sophocles, Plato, Galileo, and Walt Whitman on the "hell list" that he had emphatically presented to his congregation one night in the Glory Barn. "If Mr. Sunday believes there is a hell," said Isadora, "I advise him to go there, where he may speak with more authority."[3]

As usual, Billy ignored them all. He had encountered criticism ever since he had begun preaching back in Garner, Iowa. Journalists such as H. L. Mencken, Henry M. Tichenor, and Charles Erskine Scott Wood, as well as many well-known clergymen, had ridiculed him as an uneducated, money-hungry huckster and bigot. Carl Sandburg wrote a poem in 1915 called "To a Contemporary Bunkshooter," in which he openly parodied Billy as a con man.

"The employer that makes the working man work for wages that keep him on the verge of starvation and don't begin to pay him for the labor he expends is a thief," Billy had stated in a 1915 address in Philadelphia. "So is the working man that doesn't give his employer an honest return for the wages he gets a thief."[4] However, prominent labor advocates such as Emma Goldman refused to believe that Billy truly cared about the everyday worker. Goldman organized a campaign in Paterson, New Jersey, at the same time as Billy's 1915 crusade. Brilliant, bitter, and deeply concerned about the terrible plight of many workers whose employers gave lip service to Billy's views, Emma declared that laborers needed better treatment, not insane blather about theology. Her fellow labor advocate and lover, Dr. Ben Reitman, concluded her impassioned speeches with this prayer: "Now, Mr. God, I don't want to make you tired by asking too much. Some of us who do not want to meet you face to face and walk on the golden streets want to get the full product of our labor. We want to build a world where we can live in beauty, harmony and freedom. If you can help us, Mr. God, we will be much obliged, and if you don't we will help ourselves and you can devote more of your time to Billy Sunday. Amen."[5]

That night, Turn Hall, the scene of the Goldman rally, burned down. Billy issued no statements regarding the fire, but many of his supporters saw the fire as a direct punishment of those who would defy God. Emma Goldman left town and was later deported to Russia for her activities.

Not only had Billy been attacked verbally, he sometimes fended off physical assaults. He had just begun his sermon in Springfield, Illinois, when a burly man named Sherman Potts charged toward the platform, wildly swinging a whip, bellowing that God had commissioned him to punish the evangelist.

Billy did not panic in the least. "I have a commission from God to knock the tar out of you, you lobster!"[6] He leaped down from the pulpit and injured his ankle but beat his assailant with his fists until others subdued Potts completely. Billy resumed his sermon (without his usual dives, jumps, and whirls), but later admitted that perhaps it was just as well his ankle prevented him from dealing with the man as he wanted. The old instincts from his baseball years came back too easily.

*I'm more than ready if some mutt here in New York gets a revelation from God to do me in.* Billy grinned wickedly as he and Nell continued their planning session, but he tried to turn his attention to the task at hand.

Nell pushed a stack of letters toward him. "Billy, there are more bad ones today." She tried not to let her lip tremble. Nell had trusted God implicitly during long periods of poverty and uncertainty. She trusted Him now. But the caustic hatred that poured from each page of the letters seemed to ignite the very air. Two even threatened Billy Sunday with death.

"Those? Give 'em to the police. They'll take care of it. Why, Nell, I got a few thousand others on my desk telling me what a great guy I am. Mrs. Sunday, ma'am, did you know you're married to a perfect man?"

She couldn't help laughing at his twinkling eyes, but her own dark ones did not absorb the mirth. "I'm glad there are so many policemen at each meeting." Armies of uniformed officers had directed the crowds outside the tabernacle every night, many of them seating themselves among the congregation close to the platform. Others maintained an obvious presence around the Sundays' hotel.

"The city's promised to make sure everyone's safe," Billy assured her, holding her cold hand. Billy himself did not realize some of his powerful friends quietly kept an eye on him. A supporter in the Justice Department in

Washington, D.C., had sent two agents posing as newspapermen to guard him during the Emma Goldman affair—something neither Billy nor Nell ever discovered.

"God's got his angels working overtime to take care of me," said Billy. "At least, that's what my ma used to say when I was little."

Nell tried to nod confidently, then handed him a much bigger pile of letters. He rolled his eyes in dismay.

Now it was Nell's turn to grin. Billy looked exactly like their son Paul had when, at the age of six, he denounced school as a place where "they didn't give me nothing to do; only to just sit there. And I can't waste my time that way."[7]

Billy rifled impatiently through the huge heap of letters, kissed Nell loudly, then bounded out the door to his meetings.

He had no idea that the force that would attack during the New York crusade would not hurt him, but Nell. In early May he rushed Ma Sunday to the hospital with acute appendicitis. Billy was beside himself with worry and fear. Nell had never gotten sick; she was the indefatigable nurse who hopped trains home to care for George through his surgery or help Willie recuperate from a broken leg. She was, as George had addressed her in one of his letters, the "General Manager, General Fixer, General All-Around Healer of the Troubles of the World."[8] How could Ma, the all-sufficient manager of the Billy Sunday crusades, become ill? Billy prayed for his wife as he rode to appointments, ate dinner with distinguished supporters, even as he preached to the New York crowds every night. He, as well as crusade audiences, cheered wildly when George read daily reports of her rapid recovery.

"Ma, I'm never going to take you for granted again,"

Billy told his wife as he brought yet another huge bouquet of roses into her hospital room.

"If you do, I guess I'll have to grow another appendix to take out," teased Nell.

Billy looked at her so seriously that she stopped joking. "I can't tell you what you mean to me," he said.

> Brighten the corner where you are,
> Brighten the corner where you are,
> Someone far from harbor you may guide across the bar,
> Brighten the corner where you are.

The throng of well-wishers sang their good-byes, with the words of Ina Duley Ogdon's popular gospel song. The crowd waved handkerchiefs and threw flowers as the train carrying Billy and his entourage pulled out of Penn Station. Billy's career records shattered when almost seventy-five thousand New Yorkers attended the three meetings on his last day, June 17, 1917. He had bonded with New York in a way he had never expected. He'd rather hold a crusade in that city than be president, he declared.

But now the familiar exhaustion began to sink upon him like a lowering ceiling. Billy had eaten and slept erratically throughout the crusade, especially during Nell's illness. He had spoken several times a day, but Billy's speaking involved more physical effort than most preaching. Some estimated that during an average urban campaign, Billy jogged, leaped, spun, fell, shadowboxed, and walked 150 miles. For six nights out of seven, for ten weeks straight, he had shaken thousands of hands.

"Billy, do you want to go to the dining car?"

"I'm not sure I could lift a fork, Nell."

She hustled him to their sleeping car. The city, with its tall buildings and dirty streets, would soon give way to the lush green fields and quiet towns of the Midwest. Other than for her illness, Nell had enjoyed every moment of the exciting New York crusade. But now Nell was ready for auto rides in the tranquil Indiana countryside, picnics along the lake with Paul, and even a little golf with her husband. *We can't get to Winona Lake fast enough, Lord.*

# FIFTEEN

B illy can't sit still for a moment!" Nell watched her
husband through the kitchen window and shook
her head.

Helen smiled at her mother as the two finished the
noontime dishes. Helen was a lovely young woman with a
gentle, quiet demeanor. While Nell loved her three ram-
bunctious sons, her relationship with her daughter was a
special one. Throughout Helen's college years, the two had
carried on a voluminous correspondence. Nell enjoyed the
times Helen and her husband, Mark, left their Sturgis,
Michigan, home to stay at "Mt. Hood" for a weekend.

"The old daddy just has to do *something*," Helen
agreed. Billy had donned his old clothes and a Panama
hat and was trimming the shrubbery vigorously.

"He'll mow the grass again. He just mowed it three
days ago!" lamented Nell.

Helen laughed. "Maybe we can go for a drive before
supper."

"I don't know if that's a good idea," said Nell, grinning at her daughter. The word *leisurely* did not exist in Billy's vocabulary. The last time he had taken them for a ride, he had used every ounce of his ample charm to talk a policeman out of issuing him a speeding ticket.

"Daddy has to relax *sometime*," insisted Helen.

"He'll never be one to sit around," said Nell. "Who is that strange man?"

"Probably a reporter," said Helen. She and her brothers were used to their father's fame.

"He has a camera!" Nell dried her hands energetically and headed for the door. "Your father is *not* having his picture taken in those clothes!"

Helen smiled as Ma Sunday tried to persuade Billy to change out of his ragged pants and faded shirt.

*Old Daddy will resist, but Ma will win out. She always does.*

Helen's face paled as a familiar pain shot through her head and drained her strength. *Not today, God, please, not today. I don't want Ma and Daddy to worry about me today.*

Helen knew her parents' concerns nearly crushed them at times. Her father's incredibly successful crusade career had consumed their every waking moment. Sometimes Helen almost physically felt the weight of their stress as she entered their house. Sermons, converts, schedules, contacts, finances—how did they survive it all?

Her parents also worried about her brothers. *With good reason*, Helen thought. *I resented being the oldest; when I was growing up, Daddy wasn't famous. Ma made me study and behave. There was no money for the luxuries the boys take for granted. But now I can see I had it better than they did.*

She and George had always been close. They had carried on a steady correspondence throughout their lonely college and boarding-school days, consoling each other when their parents could not attend a special school event or arrive home in time for Christmas. *When the old daddy could not make it to my graduation, George was the one who made me smile.* Helen often addressed him as "Psyche." When he was in his teens, she had warned him to beware of "Syrian maidens." "Have as good a time as you can but don't do anything you will be ashamed of."[1] George had often scandalized Winona Lake with his escapades. Because of his father's unique position, he felt himself above everyday rules. Now twenty-five and married to Harriet Mason, George showed no signs of settling down. He regularly charmed his way out of trouble, as he always had.

Billy Jr., often inspired polite but dismayed letters from his teachers. The headmaster at his New Jersey boarding school wrote Billy Sr., that his sixteen-year-old son would not be allowed to keep his new Buick at school. Billy Jr., he commented, was an extremely likeable young man, with an ability to pick up information quickly, but "when Mrs. Sunday and yourself could not be there [home], he has not had very strict supervision. But what he lacks most of all is to learn to live a quiet life, and to form good habits of work. . . ."[2] Billy Sr., managed his son's infractions as best he could over long distances, but Helen knew that when Billy Jr., responded with repentant promises to do better, the teenager forgot about them the minute he dropped the letter into the mailbox.

Nine-year-old Paul appeared quiet, like herself, but Helen knew the youngest Sunday boy possessed a relentless appetite for action, like his older brothers.

Helen laughed softly as she watched her father shrug resignedly and trudge toward the house as Nell spoke animatedly with the reporter. *They're quite a pair!*

She dried the last dish. *They're not perfect. Sometimes they've hurt me more than they know, with their being so busy and so wrapped up in each other. But I know they love me. And they love the boys.* Helen hung up the dish towel, then slowly, painfully, made her way to a chair in the parlor.

Several months later, Billy touched the train window with one finger. To his surprise, it did not freeze his hand.

"We really are in the South, aren't we?" he said to Nell.

"Many of the trees are still green," answered Ma Sunday. She savored the sunshine and the rural countryside that flowed past them as the *Dixie Flyer* sped toward Atlanta. "You'd never know it's November, would you?"

She rejoiced to see Billy talking confidently with the reporters who, as always, swarmed throughout their railroad car. For some time he had wrestled with his decision to conduct a crusade in Atlanta.

The son of a Union soldier who died during the Civil War, he had displayed reluctance to hold revivals in the South. A staunch Republican, he found it difficult to identify with the largely Democratic South.

Billy also had struggled with racial issues. He personally believed that God viewed blacks and whites as equals, and he publicly denounced the lynchings and violence that often plagued the South at the turn of the twentieth century. But, like most white Christians of his era, he was not convinced that blacks were on the same level with whites socially.

He himself knew few blacks. Professional baseball did not allow black players when Billy played in the 1880s. His manager, Cap Anson, had declared he would remove his team from the field if the opposition dared insert a black man into their lineup. Few black people attended his crusades in the North. Billy rarely rubbed shoulders with blacks back in Winona Lake, but he had become acquainted with at least one: the Reverend Henry Hugh Proctor, the pastor of Atlanta's First Congregational Church. Rev. Proctor had spoken at the Winona Lake Conference Center about "The Attitude of the Colored People towards Temperance in the South." Afterwards Billy shook the speaker's hand and complimented him on his lecture.

"Why don't you come to Atlanta, Brother Sunday?" asked the Reverend Proctor. "You would find many open hearts among us." He smiled. "And I can guarantee you will hear some of the most beautiful music you ever heard on God's earth."

Billy pondered the possibility for weeks. *Are you calling me to Atlanta, Lord?* He and Nell prayed, then shared the idea with their staff.

Billy and his assistants grappled with the practical issues involved in holding crusades in cities that rigidly enforced the twenty-year-old Supreme Court decision that permitted separation of the races in neighborhoods, buses, restaurants, hotels—and churches.

*Should we hold meetings for everyone together and set up special galleries for blacks?* That approach, Billy knew, would create such outrage among whites that it would vaporize any attempts at evangelization.

*Or should we follow the usual Southern custom and conduct separate but equal meetings?* Billy knew that Dwight L. Moody, the famed Chicago evangelist, had held revivals in the South in the past, designating specific nights for black worshipers.

*What is the best thing to do, Lord?* Billy agonized

about the racial dilemma for days.

Finally, he and his staff had decided to hold separate revivals for blacks and whites in Atlanta. That issue resolved, Billy began to anticipate the Atlanta crusade with his usual energy and enthusiasm.

Southern hospitality had already made its mark on Billy. Many who had read of his efforts in the northern cities gathered at the train stations to cheer the famous evangelist. Field workers and small-town folks, recognizing Billy's train, waved at the *Dixie Flyer* as she rumbled past. A Chattanooga railway worker had presented Billy with an original poem called "Can a Trainman Be a Christian?" in honor of his new venture. The widow of Sam Jones, a prominent southern evangelist, greeted Billy in Nashville.

Now, as the train pulled into the Atlanta station, a huge throng of enthusiastic supporters and curious on-lookers, along with the ever-present army of journalists and photographers, welcomed Billy Sunday and his entourage. A well-wisher filled Nell's arms with chrysanthemums.

*Such a wonderful, friendly place.* The cordial, gracious smiles—how could this be the same place where all that killing had taken place? Only ten years before, in 1907, Billy had read about rioting whites who had attacked blacks in their own Atlanta neighborhoods. Terrified men, women, and children had taken refuge wherever they could; many hid on the campuses of several black universities in the area. Not all escaped the fury of the mob. Ten black people had died, and many had been badly hurt. Businesses and homes had been burned to the ground. The madness halted only when the governor sent in the state militia.

Billy shook his head in consternation and grief, but he turned his attention to the matter at hand. *If Atlantans truly come to Christ, they will have a charitable attitude toward each other.*

His crusade organization had, as usual, done a superb job preparing for the meetings. On November 4, 1917, twelve thousand people jammed the new tabernacle at the corner of Jackson and Irwin streets, where a big circus tent had once stood. Georgia's governor, the mayor of Atlanta, and other prominent city politicians, clergymen, and society women attended Billy's first meeting, along with tradesmen and shopkeepers, office girls and baseball fans.

Billy did not disappoint them. He clowned until the tabernacle rocked with laughter. Southern preachers spoke freely of hell, but Billy made his audience hear the crackle and feel the searing heat of the flames. He boxed Satan, who tried to slither away from God's fearless warrior. He thumped his pulpit, slid into nonexistent bases and caught imaginary balls in deep center field, roared and ranted—and his congregation loved it all. Billy's sermons, printed in full by the *Atlanta Constitution* every day, became the talk of the city.

As usual, Billy immersed himself in knowing the area. He visited Stone Mountain and other tourist sites; he mixed with public officials and clergy, speaking and socializing every opportunity he got. He and his staff made it a priority to lay the groundwork for the blacks-only meetings that would soon begin.

First, Billy met with black civil and religious leaders, involving them in the planning of their crusade. Such joint cooperation between Christian blacks and whites was unprecedented in the South.

Several black colleges (Morehouse, Spellman, Clark

University, Atlanta University, Atlanta Baptist College, and Fisk University) flourished in the city. A growing class of educated blacks, including activists Professor John Hope and W. E. B. Dubois, an originator of the National Association for the Advancement of Colored People, pointed the way to a better future for Atlanta's blacks.

Yet most lived in wretched poverty. Racism in every form abounded throughout the city, with Jim Crow laws enforced to the fullest extent. Books such as *The Negro: A Beast; The Negro: A Menace to American Civilization;* and *The Clansman* (on which the film *The Birth of a Nation* was based) were popular in Atlanta.

Would black people who lived under those conditions trust a white preacher?

On November 19, 1917, fifteen thousand black worshipers packed the Billy Sunday tabernacle. Journalists estimated this crowd to be the largest black group ever gathered in the South. College professors and their pupils, weary workmen in overalls, ministers, military personnel from Camp Gordon, domestic workers, and black community organizations filled the wooden benches. Aged former slaves marveled at the opportunity to hear a famous white evangelist. Another whole congregation stood outside in the pouring rain, straining to hear Billy Sunday.

First Rody led the opening hymn, "My Country, 'Tis of Thee." The choir, composed of a thousand young men and women mostly from various colleges in the area, led the congregation, and together they sang as no crusade audience had ever sung. A group from Morris Brown College sang a rhythmic, passionate version of "Morris Brown Gonna Shine Tonight." Rody was so mesmerized by the special number that he asked them to sing it two more times. Then a young woman from Clark University rose to sing "Swing Low, Sweet Chariot," in a rich, sweet voice, with the choir echoing behind her.

Billy decided the Reverend Proctor had been absolutely right. This was the most beautiful music he would ever hear on God's earth.

But when the choir and congregation sang one of Billy's favorites, "Down by the Riverside," with the bass section spontaneously rising to sing deep, deep down low, he almost felt his feet leave the floor.

*It's angel music, Lord. That has to be the way the angels sing.*

The congregation sang and sang, well into the evening.

Then the crowd rustled expectantly as Billy rose to address them.

His early remarks received polite attention, but little else. He noted Booker T. Washington's accomplishments and praised the hard work and perseverance of blacks in Atlanta. They had made amazing progress since the Civil War because they lived among whites who appreciated their loyalty during the war, when many soldiers left their families with faithful black servants. Most blacks and whites minded their own business as decent, law-abiding citizens. The violence that occasionally broke out nowadays was the work of evil malcontents and extremists on both sides.

Billy had not anticipated the quiet.

He swallowed a little, then shed his coat, collar, and tie and began to preach from his well-worn Bible.

King David of the Old Testament was not a man after God's own heart because he was perfect, Billy declared. He was God's man because he repented of his sin. No one, black or white, would go to heaven unless he knelt before Almighty God in humility, confessing his sin honestly.

Billy had visited the black colleges, probing the desires and difficulties of the young people and their teachers. He had studied black workers, professionals, and businessmen throughout Atlanta, trying to familiarize himself with their beliefs, customs, and methods of communication.

Now he told stories of Old Testament prophets so vibrantly, he almost made them appear on the platform beside him, clad in sackcloth and ashes. The prophets' dusty beards dripped with sweat as Billy's own face did; they pointed with him at a congregation that needed to turn to God. Their eyes flashed together at the nauseating blandness of contemporary religion. Their voices pleaded in unison for a return to the passion of truly knowing God.

His audience sat stunned for only a moment. Soon cries of "Hallelujah!" and "Preach it, Brother!" resounded throughout the tabernacle. Billy shouted and raged; his black brothers and sisters shouted and raged. Billy whispered; the worshipers sent back quiet echoes of "Lord have mercy" and "Yessir, yessir." Billy laughed and cried with joy as he visualized the Good Shepherd bringing home one lost lamb; his listeners celebrated with him. "Amen! Amen! Glory to God!"

By the end of the sermon, men, women, and children burst toward the altar as if a dam had broken. Billy clasped their hands gladly, his red face wet with perspiration and tears.

The next all-black meeting was not scheduled until December 1. "We can't wait that long to hear that choir again," Billy told Rody. "Let's have them sing for one of the white meetings."

Rody nodded. Although he had heard many skilled, talented musical groups, this choir moved him like no other.

Many feared the whites might boycott such a blatant disregard for racial rules, but the success of the black meeting piqued the curiosity of Atlanta's whites. They showed up by the thousands.

The sight of a thousand black college students gathered at the front of the tabernacle overwhelmed them a little. But when the choir sang their poignant spirituals, weaving harmonies into an effortless tapestry of sound, then shaking the walls of the tabernacle with their powerful music, the audience sat hypnotized. After the service they hastened to compliment the musicians. One young black woman who had sung in the choir marveled at the multitude of white hands she had shaken. Eventually the black choir grew to six thousand members, as singers from Wheat Street Baptist, Mount Olive, Mount Zion, Big Bethel, and other Atlanta churches joined the college students to fill the tabernacle and the city blocks outside with their haunting hymns and swinging spirituals.

Billy continued to preach as he had for years. He denounced moral looseness and sinful entertainments. He thundered out the wrath of God against alcohol consumption and suppliers. He affirmed the importance of family life, hard work, and good citizenship.

Most of all, Billy spoke of man's relationship with God and his need to repent.

He continued his campaign against the Kaiser, calling for selfless patriotism among Americans. One night, as he vilified the Germans for their brutality, W. H. Beuterbaugh, a German-American carpenter, charged at Billy, swinging his fists. Billy easily fended off the attack with several well-aimed punches. The peaceful euphoria that had ruled his Atlanta crusade exploded into anarchy, with many terrified people running for the exits and others joining in the fray. Some screamed, "Kill! Lynch him!" An unknown assailant tried to strangle the mayor of Atlanta during the fight. Although unrelated to black/white issues, the incident seemed to resurrect an uneasy ghost of savagery.

As the Atlanta crusade drew to a close just before Christmas 1917, many blacks and whites affirmed the positive effects of the Billy Sunday crusade. Dr. Adam Williams ministered at Ebenezer Baptist Church, where Martin Luther King Sr., and his son later served. He celebrated the improved atmosphere of the city, his own spiritual growth, and even a repentant debtor's repayment of money owed to him. Perhaps he had better search out his other debtors, he quipped to the tabernacle congregation, before this revival ended.

The Reverend P. James Bryant of Wheat Street Baptist, an accomplished orator who represented the Colored Evangelical Ministers Union, gently parodied Billy's famous addiction to adjectives when he said Billy was a "hypnotic, dynamic, athletic, linguistic, spellbinding gospel expounder," and thanked him "for the service he has rendered our community and for the sagacious, orthodox, evangelical, ethical, and intensely practical gospel message he has delivered to us as a race."[3]

The Reverend Henry Alford Porter, of Atlanta's white Second Baptist Church, declared that all Atlanta should express gratitude that Billy Sunday had come to preach the gospel. City officials rejoiced at the drop in crime and violence that had accompanied the revival. Clergymen, educators, parents, long-suffering spouses—black and white—blessed the day Billy Sunday entered their city.

Billy and Nell left Atlanta to the usual accompaniment of tears, cheers, and hymn singing and headed home to Winona Lake for Christmas.

Billy and Nell long remembered the power of worshiping with black brothers and sisters, the sharing of a common joy in salvation and a promised eternity in heaven together. Later Billy tried to describe the sweetness of "Amazing Grace" rising from six thousand black throats. He told of singing "Ain't Gonna Study War No More" with black pastors on the platform.

Soon, however, he spoke of it less and less. Some of Billy's friends expressed concern that a focus on joint black/white ministry would threaten his support base and thus make it impossible for him to accomplish his primary goal: to save as many souls as possible. While Billy saw no gray areas in matters involving alcohol, sex, and patriotism, he regarded racial issues in a different light. When the Billy Sunday tabernacle went up in Richmond, Virginia, the following year, no blacks were invited to attend—an insult that enraged the editors of the *Richmond Planet*, a black newspaper. When Billy, in an effort to calm the storm, invited Richmond blacks to fill the balconies one night only, the *Planet* urged them to stay home. All but twenty-one of them did.

Billy later conducted all-black services in his Wichita and Kansas City crusades. While other white evangelists avoided black churches as if they did not exist, he sometimes filled their pulpits. He crossed racial lines when no other evangelist of his era dared do so.

Billy would not join hands and hearts with his black friends, as he had in Atlanta, until they all walked together where Jim Crow could not follow them.

# SIXTEEN

I believe God is going to send me to France next summer!" The Washington, D.C., congregation, which included many soldiers soon to board troopships bound for the war in Europe, whooped and hollered with glee.

Billy wanted to minister in the trenches, spending time with the boys on the front lines, many of whom he regarded as his friends. "After all, I've preached to half of the soldiers we've sent," Billy declared.

"I'd like a chance to shoot at the Kaiser myself," Billy Sunday deadpanned. "But if he won't face me like a man, I guess I'll have to point a rifle at some of his dirty German buddies!"

Nell watched her husband persuade his audience to invest in Liberty Bonds. "Don't show up at my meetings again until you've bought a bond!" *He'll buy some more tomorrow,* she mused. Nell and Billy had invested twenty-five thousand dollars in Liberty Bonds during the New York revival; she had no doubt he was prepared to loan more money to the government.

*He means every word he says,* she thought, half proudly, half regretfully. Nell knew Billy had already laid the groundwork for his departure to Europe, discussing the details with Washington officials. YMCA leaders, military authorities, and powerful friends like John D. Rockefeller Jr., had all urged Billy to go.

*He may be middle-aged,* thought Nell, *but he has more energy and nerve than most of those raw boys on the troopships. Lord Jesus, how they need Billy right now. . . .* She watched the smooth young faces of hundreds of recruits, their eyes wild and eager.

When the Sunday crusade organization had arrived in Washington in January, the nation's early enthusiasm for World War I had waned. Fervent prowar editorials in the newspapers had given way to growing lists of those killed and wounded in action. Sullen citizens ignored the meatless and wheatless days espoused by the government, and appeals to buy Liberty Bonds fell on near-deaf ears.

All that changed when Billy Sunday came to town.

He ripped through the heavy clouds of apathy like a knight on a white charger, brandishing his razor-sharp rhetoric. God had anointed America to stop the atrocities in Europe, so she had better get to work! He met with the House of Representatives, leading them in a prayer that God would help defeat the vicious, greedy, evil Germans. The startled congressmen exploded into applause as Billy shook hands and slapped shoulders. Spectators in the gallery rose to cheer and clap. Speaker of the House Champ Clark pounded his gavel to no avail.

Billy began making rounds of Washington officials. He met with Newton Baker, the secretary of war, and

Josephus Daniels, the secretary of the navy. Soon Billy was calling treasury secretary William McAdoo "Mac." Eventually he visited the White House, where President Wilson lauded his patriotic record and thanked him for his support.

When the chairman of the United States Shipping Board, Edward N. Hurley, asked Billy to help convince shipbuilders to discontinue their wartime strike, Billy immediately declared in his sermons that such self-centeredness undermined national interests. Godly citizens, he insisted, supported the government during wartime; they did not tear the country apart by greed. With the help of Samuel Gompers and other labor officials, the workers began building ships once more, and Billy celebrated a victory against what he saw as a German plot to ruin United States sea power.

Billy offered his Washington, D.C., tabernacle as a temporary shelter for incoming soldiers and bought cots and provisions for them out of his own funds. He invited the United States Fuel Administration to promote the conservation of coal at his tabernacle meetings.

Billy lobbied for the war effort in every possible way. No patriotic act was too big or too small, no sacrifice too demanding. Although now in his fifties, he dared risk his own safety by going to Europe to inspire the young men around him.

But President Wilson's newest request left him as limp as a tossed-aside rag doll.

When Billy announced his intention to go to Europe to fight the evil Huns, the White House issued an immediate invitation for a conference. President Wilson told him his assistance at home was invaluable. Billy had accomplished the impossible in Washington since his arrival: He had transformed a listless, war-weary people into zealous patriots. "We have plenty of people who inspire and entertain the soldiers overseas," said the president. "But no one can do what you have done here at home. We need you. Please remain here in America."

Four months later the president would refuse to appoint Billy to an international committee on prisoner exchange in Berne, Switzerland, despite his eager desire to serve. While Wilson valued Billy's influence over Americans, he evidently doubted his foreign diplomatic abilities, especially since Billy nightly affirmed his ambition to shoot at Kaiser Bill.

As a loyal citizen-soldier of his commander-in-chief, Billy agreed to give up his dreams of heroism in Europe. Billy's midnight pacing in the parlor, his diminished appetite, the caged-bird look in his eyes all reminded Nell too much of his frustration as a young YMCA office worker in Chicago.

*Billy, you never were good at playing it safe.* Nell soothed his irritability, then pushed her husband back into action, knowing that was the best antidote for his frustrations. Despite his disappointment at Wilson's dictate, Billy doubled his usual hectic pace, contacting industrial heads, lobbying politicians, speaking to civic and service organizations, challenging the people to return to Jesus Christ and support their country's holy cause. Almost every night for two months, he spoke to thousands who packed his tabernacle and stood outside in the cold for hours.

When Billy left Washington in early March 1918, he believed he had carried out the mission with which God had entrusted him. He had shared the gospel with a fearful, despairing people, giving them hope for the future and faith in God's provision during wartime. He had prepared hundreds of young soldiers to face death. He had done all he could to defeat evil, as he saw it, and support righteousness.

God's warrior needed a few weeks of rest at Winona Lake.

"Look here in the paper!" Billy thrust the headlines under Nell's nose as she drank her morning coffee. Paul and Billy Jr., who had come home for a visit, peered at the news. "Another state has ratified the resolution! God is going to rid our country forever of that evil stuff! I can feel it in my bones!"

Privately, Billy Jr., had his doubts. Too many of his friends drank every weekend, all weekend. Alcohol was a way of life for Billy Jr., himself. *Whether it's legal or not, we'll find ways to get it.* Paul, his younger brother, continued wolfing down his toast and marmalade as his father rejoiced. Paul glanced at Billy Jr., then dropped his eyes. Did his father really think Paul would not encounter booze when he went to college? Had he no idea that their brother George drank heavily?

But he said nothing. Nell's sharp, dark eyes had already fixed on Billy Jr., and he dared not incriminate himself. His father desperately needed his rest when he came home to Winona Lake. Billy Sr., rarely detected any problems with his children. He spent as much time as possible with them but left the rest to Nell, just as he did his crusades. Now the evangelist celebrated his certain victory against alcohol with a big bowl of strawberries smothered in fresh cream.

"Those look awfully good," Billy Jr., told his mother. "Bet they cost a lot less than we pay in the city."

Nell beamed. She spooned more strawberries into bowls and insisted her sons sample them as she told them how little she'd had to pay for several big bucketfuls. "If you just pick them yourself, they're only four cents a quart." People had to work at it, Nell insisted, if they wanted to save money. Nell, who even at the height of her husband's financial success asked for the leftovers after elegant dinners, loved a bargain above all else.

Billy Jr., munched the sweet berries and chuckled inwardly. His mother, unlike his father, usually detected the guilty when she was at home, dealing out discipline coolly and efficiently, but Billy had realized long ago that the best way to distract Ma from his own sins was to fix her attention on saving money.

*I haven't lost my touch, Ma.*

Victory in Europe! The soldiers were coming home! Billy, Nell, and the crusade staff celebrated Armistice Day, November 11, 1918, with the same frenzy that swept the country. Billy exulted as he saw good defeat evil once more. But even "Kaiser Bill's" downfall did not give him the same satisfaction that another victory gave Billy in January 1919.

Three-fourths of the states ratified the Eighteenth Amendment. Prohibition became law.

The day before it went into effect in January 1920, Billy and his friends created a funeral for John Barleycorn in Norfolk, Virginia, complete with a twenty-foot black coffin, pallbearers, and a red-clad Satan who appeared to grieve deeply about the demise of his best friend. Throngs of supporters cheered as the procession passed by. Fifteen thousand of them squeezed into Billy's tabernacle, where the evangelist preached a blistering sermon, pulling out all the stops. John Barleycorn had trapped innocent people, murdered them, destroyed their families! But now he was dead, and Billy, for one, would not mourn his passing. The crowd hurrahed in approval and sang "John Barleycorn's Body Lies a Mouldering in the Clay." Three little girls brought Billy and Nell bouquets of white roses and carnations. Billy and Nell even sang an off-key duet in honor of the occasion, to the audience's great amusement, since they were well acquainted with the Sundays' self-admitted lack of musical ability. Billy brought them to their feet by standing on his pulpit, waving a huge American flag. "Let's sing the Doxology!" he roared, and the congregation belted out the closing song, but not loudly enough to drown out Billy's unharmonious voice.

No one cared. God had triumphed! Sin was defeated! God's soldier, who had tirelessly worked for the downfall of this vile Goliath, now celebrated, like the Old Testament King David, with all his might.

# SEVENTEEN

We have bootleggers on every corner, gamblers, thieves, murderers, and your women are insulted and debauched. . .our best citizens are breaking the law without compunction,"[1] Colonel John Baker White, who led the Law and Order League of Kanawha County, West Virginia, wrote Billy Sunday not long after Prohibition. He plainly felt the country's moral fiber was deteriorating.

Billy could only concur with his friend's evaluation of 1920s society.

Colonel White not only despaired of the country's general moral climate, he lamented the total lack of conscience exhibited by not only the poor and uneducated, but by the upstanding citizens of his area. Everyone seemed to employ his own personal bootlegger. Businessmen, officials, teachers, even judges ignored the dictates of the Eighteenth Amendment.

*How can they do it, Lord?* Billy cried. *How can they scorn an amendment of the United States Constitution and get away with it?* He preached against alcohol with renewed venom, and his tabernacle congregations affirmed him with loud amens, but the speakeasies and the corruption that accompanied them grew steadily.

Billy's dynamic power to attract and influence huge audiences brought his name to the fore during the election of 1920. Some Republican leaders had toyed with the possibility of his running for president or vice president throughout the past successful years of Billy's career, especially when he and his supporters helped bring about the upset win during the dry/wet resolution controversy in Michigan in 1916. Billy himself half-jokingly announced a cabinet he would form if elected. Not surprisingly, it included Ma Sunday as a possible candidate for secretary of state. The chairman of the Prohibition party, W. G. Calder-Wood, pushed hard for a ticket consisting of William Jennings Bryan and Billy Sunday, but the plan never jelled. The day before the Prohibition convention convened in Lincoln, Nebraska, Billy, who had retreated to his Oregon ranch, declared his support for Republican Warren G. Harding. William Jennings Bryan affirmed his support for the Democratic party, which he had served for years.

When his possible political ambitions came to naught, Billy turned anew to his crusade career. He often spoke to immense audiences in large cities, as he had for the past ten to fifteen years, but they did not compare to the earlier crusades in New York, Atlanta, and Washington, D.C. His Chicago revival in the spring of 1918, which he had particularly anticipated, did not match his past campaigns in fervor or results. More and more the evangelist found himself speaking in Knoxville, Tennessee, and Louisville, Kentucky, and even in smaller cities such as Aurora, Illinois, and Fairmont, West Virginia. He received fewer invitations from the East Coast urban areas and the West.

Even his native Midwest did not welcome Billy with the same unbridled enthusiasm; by the 1920s, most had either heard or read his sermons.

*I want to go wherever You send me, Lord. I want to see souls come to Christ wherever I preach. But, Lord. . .am I slipping? Am I doing something wrong?*

Second-rate imitators and outright con men tried to achieve Billy's success. They succeeded mostly in shrinking Billy's audiences.

Billy had not focused on the South until the 1917 Atlanta revival. During the 1920s, he often conducted crusades in the strongly fundamentalist southern states, where the population still lauded his fiery, uncompromising message of sin, repentance, and salvation through a personal relationship with Jesus Christ. More and more, Billy felt at home in the South.

But the sixty-year-old preacher mostly found his postwar world a bewildering, distressing puzzle.

The burgeoning entertainment industry had caught the nation's attention. Glamorous film stars, not evangelists, captured the public's imagination. Billy bluntly denounced the immorality that pervaded Hollywood lifestyles, but most shrugged at such old-fashioned values.

Soldiers returning from World War I no longer wanted to stay down on the farm or spend their Saturday nights at crusade meetings. An economic boom contributed to people's obsession with pleasure and material success. Quite simply, they wanted to spend their money on themselves, not religious work.

Even the Christian network of churches that Billy

had loved, criticized, and brought together for so many years had changed radically. When he planned a crusade in previous years, Billy had depended heavily on a united community of Protestant pastors and laymen who believed that God had sent His divine Son to die for humanity's sins. Billy Sunday, they were convinced, was His messenger, preaching from God's infallible book, the Bible. Their parishioners, neighbors, and relatives needed to come to the crusades. They needed to repent and establish a relationship with Jesus Christ, who would teach them to care for their families, work hard, and live righteously.

The trickle of liberalism that Billy had decried throughout his ministry had invaded the country like a modern Noah's flood in the 1920s. Darwinism, a little-known theory that initially had been ignored by most Americans, now challenged creation as depicted in Genesis. Many seminary professors and pastors no longer regarded the Bible as the standard for their theological beliefs. Others refused to accept the supernatural in their biblical texts, insisting that Jesus' divinity was unfounded and His virgin birth and miracles allegorical, not literal. They wanted nothing to do with a supposedly substitutionary, bloody death to pay for men's sins. Jesus' teachings, they declared, were the important thing. If Billy wanted to preach a "social gospel" in which followers of Christ fed the hungry, educated the ignorant, improved working conditions, and implemented social justice, very well. If he insisted on the embarrassment of repentance from sin or the historical existence of a divine Savior, they wanted nothing to do with his fundamentalist views.

"That bald-headed old mutt!"[2] Billy roared one

186

evening to Nell as she was putting supper on the table. Nell knew better than to try to soothe him. Her husband had been reading the popular views of Washington Gladden, a Congregational minister in Columbus, Ohio. Gladden, a sincere activist who saw drunkenness and immorality as symptoms of an unjust culture, had aroused Billy's ire more than once. Gladden and other Social Gospel proponents such as Rochester Theological Seminary professor Walter Rauschenbusch; Herbert Newton of All Souls Church in New York City; Francis Peabody, a Harvard faculty member; and W. S. Rainsford, a self-described "Christian communist," minimized the importance of winning souls to Christ while emphasizing the creation of a new society that would mirror the kingdom of heaven.

"Nell, Gladden's leading people straight to hell! No one cares about poor people more than God does. But He cares most of all about their souls, where they're going to spend all eternity! These eggheaded sissies would fill their bellies, then empty their minds of all sense!" Billy was so furious, he could not eat his dinner that evening.

Billy had preached against such newfangled theology for years. "We are as good as we are now not because of these new fads but because of the impetus of the old belief of our grandmothers and grandfathers in God and the Bible that has carried into our day."[3]

In 1926, Collier's magazine had invited both Billy Sunday, the famous fundamentalist, and the Reverend A. Wakefield Slaten, the pastor of the West Side Unitarian Church of New York City, to write side-by-side articles defining the current spiritual climate and asking each whether fundamentalist Christianity would survive.

Slaten believed that Americans were finally sounding

the death knell of the uncivilized Christian myths that had permeated their culture far too long. Educated people, he asserted, now knew that Jesus Christ had only been a man and that God was an impersonal force. Their descendants would learn to pursue harmonious, productive lives through the power of intellectual pursuit and evolutionary development.

As usual, Billy made his answer abundantly clear: "BLAH!" to liberal theologians and empty-headed intellectuals! "BUNK!" to godless artists and musicians, lewd entertainment, and blasphemous theories such as evolution!⁴ Americans, he asserted, might go through a time of exploration, even extreme confusion, but they would return to the faith of their fathers, to Jesus Christ the Son of God, who died for their sins. "Let me tell these loud-mouthed, big vocabulary, foreign-lingo slinging, quack-theory preaching bolsheviki in the pulpits and colleges that I'll put what I preach to the test any time against what they preach!"⁵

Perhaps Billy could not run, leap, whirl, and slide as he once had, but his message remained as "lean and mean" as ever. When he saw blind leaders drawing their flocks toward damnation, he trumpeted warning after warning.

His old friend, William Jennings Bryan, continued to battle liberal forces, as well. When the state of Tennessee put biology teacher John T. Scopes on trial for using a textbook that contained evolutionary material, the aged, sick warrior willingly agreed to prosecute, although he had not presented a case in a courtroom for twenty-eight years. Most observers agreed he was no match for the crafty, astute trial lawyer Clarence Darrow, a noted anti-fundamentalist who represented the American Civil Liberties Union. Darrow often trapped the elderly lawyer into looking ridiculous during the proceedings. The trial stretched into an eleven-day carnival, complete with radio coverage, hordes of reporters, curiosity seekers, and brisk souvenir sales. The trial ended with Scopes being fined a token amount for civil disobedience, but his supporters gained nationwide sympathy. Exhausted, overheated, and bewildered, Bryan died a few days later.

*Oh, Lord, I'm so sorry.* Billy could hardly believe it. The grand old man of oratory, William Jennings Bryan, dead? *I wish I could have been there to help him, Lord. Maybe my legal arguments wouldn't have amounted to much. But I sure would have enjoyed taking a punch at that Darrow fellow.* Billy fingered the telegram that informed him of Bryan's death. *He asked me to come to Tennessee for the trial.* Billy held his head in his hands.

He had not met Bryan's request because exhaustion and worry had depleted his own supply of energy.

As their children had matured, Billy and Nell had hoped this new generation of Sundays would impact their twentieth-century world for Christ, following in their parents' footsteps. When George, the oldest, became one of his father's advance men, his parents could hardly contain their joy. The young man possessed a true knack for setting up crusades. They marveled at his excellent management of key parts of the huge New York City crusade of 1917. The Sundays knew that George had exhibited a disturbing wild streak throughout his life, but surely he had sown his wild oats.

They were mistaken. George resigned from the crusade staff not long afterwards and went west to pursue a career in Los Angeles real estate. He wanted to be independent of the Sunday organization—but not independent of his father's support. Billy Sunday provided much of the capital for his new business, hoping George would focus his youthful enthusiasm on work instead of trouble. Billy Jr., soon joined his brother on the West Coast.

In November 1923, Billy and Nell, conducting a crusade in Charleston, South Carolina, received a terrifying report from Los Angeles. The *Times* reported a suicide attempt by George. Investigating officers found him unconscious, a hose stretching from a gas jet to his lips. Several hours later, conflicting accounts issued from several sources. Billy Jr., called his parents, telling them the police reports and newspaper accounts were totally ungrounded. George's pastor contradicted the police report, insisting that George, an elder in his congregation, had been afflicted somewhat with mental distress but had never attempted to take his own life. George's Swedish chauffeur told the press that Billy Jr., not his older brother, had fallen down the stairs. George himself told journalists that Billy Jr., not himself, had had an accident. Still later, his brother, looking wan and listless, would declare to reporters he had experienced severe stomach cramps after a tainted fish dinner.

Since no one had died, the Los Angeles police gave up deciphering the mystery, but the publicity surrounding the older Sunday brothers did not abate. Stories about their drinking binges, lavish lifestyles, and loose women appeared in newspapers all across the country.

"You and I are about to the end of the trail in our worries. We must get some ease from the strain or go under," Billy wrote Nell during his fall 1929 crusade in the Midwest. "It's a tragedy and all needless if the boys had obeyed our teaching and followed the Lord. George could have been my advance man to this day, and he would have met with some firm that would have discovered his ability and been in business or he could be on top out there if he had started at the bottom and learned the business, not jumped in at the top and was skinned out of all he had and most of all we had. Billy, the same way, gave himself up to evil ways and broke our hearts."[6] In another letter during the same campaign, he voiced a little hope that Billy Jr., would learn from past experience and would "keep away from that type and associate with girls of character. . . ." Perhaps he would find a suitable wife, not "these damnable gold digger lazy useless dolls. . . ."[7]

But Billy Jr., did not. *heart breaking.*

"What can we do, Ma?" asked Billy. His face, as gray and limp as his hair, hung over the newest lurid account in the *New York Times*. He sat hunched as if he were cold.

*He looks old. My Billy looks old.* Nell put her arms around her husband. After an empty pause, she answered, "We must pray, Billy. Pray that George and Billy Jr., will repent and turn back to God. Pray that others will not be hurt by their foolishness."

"How can I preach righteousness to people if my own boys turn away? Is it my fault, Nell? Did I hurt them so much?" Billy knew he had spent most of his time apart from his boys. But he remembered so many good times: skipping stones with George on Winona Lake, ice-skating with Billy Jr., at Christmas, riding horses out at the Hood River, Oregon, ranch, both boys proudly brandishing new cowboy hats. He had taught them how to catch a fly ball. They had proudly shown off his baseball paraphernalia to their friends. And how many times had they heard him preach about Jesus and repenting and holiness? He had often read to them

Jesus' parable of the Prodigal Son. . . .

"Did they ever listen, Nell? I tried to be God's man for them."

"We both tried, Billy." Her own heavy pain dulled her voice. "We're bound to have made mistakes. Maybe I should have stayed home more."

"But Nell, I couldn't have lived without you that long. I couldn't have done it all without you. Thousands of people might not be in heaven someday if we hadn't done it the way we did, Ma."

The two sat silently as the "Inglenook," a little front parlor in "Mt. Hood," darkened with the coming night. Billy put another log on the fire, and a tiny flame shot up to warm their cold, lined faces.

"God is still God," said Billy. He held Nell close on the loveseat, as he had during their courting days many years before. He still called her his "Old Lover," and "Dearest on Earth" in his letters when they were apart.[8]

"God is still God," said Billy. "And we are still us."

Convinced that God still wanted him to preach, Billy continued to speak at churches, Lions' Club meetings, and community forums. He and Nell, for the first time in years, began to face financial pressures. Both had managed their money carefully and given generously to those in need, but the shrinking crusade audiences meant smaller offerings. Not only did Billy find himself sending more and more money to his sons, but his daughter, Helen, suffered from a chronic illness (later thought to be multiple sclerosis). Her family needed money for her care. Billy tried to pack his schedule as full as he had when he was thirty-five.

In 1929, Homer Rodeheaver said good-bye to Billy's

crusade organization. Rody could no longer stomach Billy's almost desperate appeals for money during services, he said in a long letter. He loved the evangelist and sympathized with his family problems, but they had taken too great a toll on Billy Sunday. Billy did not connect with his converts as he had in the past. He no longer wanted to mix with area pastors or make the business and social contacts so vital to the success of the crusades. Perhaps it was time to stop.

Billy kept on. He preached at the Broadway Temple Methodist Episcopal Church in New York City on November 6, 1930, filling it with a thousand people, while fifty more listened outside. Despite his age and weariness, he spoke with his typical vim and vinegar, ignoring the fact that thirteen years before he had filled a twenty-thousand-seat Glory Barn with eager listeners every night.

"Repent ye, for the kingdom of heaven is at hand!" he thundered like an elderly John the Baptist and shook his fists in the air.

The nation's culture had forever changed. The America of Billy Sunday's youth, with its clear, defined beliefs, now existed only in rural areas and the South.

Billy knew these urban folk, seated in comfortable pews, resplendent in their fashionable dress, needed to come to Jesus Christ.

He would never change his message.

God was still God.

# EIGHTEEN

H as the whole country gone crazy?" Billy rattled the newspaper angrily and resumed reading. Nell knew he would not stay quiet for long. *Sometimes*, she thought, *I've thought of hiding the paper for a while, at least until Billy's had his coffee.*

"God sends America a stock market crash to let us know we've sinned as a nation. We're all looking at the bottom of the barrel. But do we repent? Of course not! No, we vote for politicians who talk about repealing Prohibition so we don't have to pay to enforce it! Besides," (here Billy adopted the "lah-di-dah" tone that he usually assigned to liberal politicians and churchmen), "we can get lots of money by taxing alcohol!" He gulped his coffee, then resumed his normal tones. "But they won't win. America won't stand for it. God won't stand for it!"

Billy continued to believe, even when anti-Prohibition forces helped pass the Twenty-First Amendment in a growing number of states. To his utter bewilderment, alcohol regained its legal status in December 1933.

That blow did not compare to the Sundays' grief at losing their daughter, Helen, the year before. Billy had been speaking throughout Michigan, trying to drum up support for Prohibition, when he and Nell were awakened by a 2:00 A.M. phone call. Their son-in-law, Mark Haines, broke the sad news. Forty-two-year-old Helen, weakened by disease and depression, had died of pneumonia. Her parents, who had been holding meetings in Detroit, found a friend who drove them through the night to Sturgis, Helen's hometown. Nell tried to comfort her young grandson, Paul. She helped Mark choose Helen's casket and plan the funeral service. Billy could not. Paralyzed by the loss of his only daughter, he told Nell he could no longer preach.

"Do you want me to cancel all your engagements?" asked Nell.

Billy said nothing.

He did, however, fill the pulpit in Waterloo, Iowa, the next meeting on his schedule, and continued his campaign throughout his native state.

Preaching—especially one-night revivals with travel in between—drained Billy's aged body and soul. But Iowa also lifted his spirits a little. He enjoyed walking the prairies once more, talking with rural pastors and their wholesome parishioners, seeing a few old friends.

One night, as he was preaching at the First Federated Church in Des Moines, Billy began to slur his words. His song leader, Harry Clarke, watched in dismay. *The boss doesn't act like he knows where he is.* The young man quickly helped Billy off the platform as the crowd fell silent. "Call a doctor!" he hissed at the ushers. Soon ambulance personnel carried Billy down the church aisle amid shocked silence, with the evangelist protesting all the way that he wanted to finish his sermon and give his hearers a chance to accept Christ. Ma Sunday insisted they take Billy to his hotel, since he disliked hospitals.

The congregation fell to its knees and prayed, many of them lingering until 4:00 A.M., imploring God to let Billy Sunday remain on earth a little longer.

With Nell's careful nursing, Billy slowly regained his strength. The heart attack would not beat him this time. His sons were relieved. "This scare may prove a blessing in disguise in that it will force him to realize a man in his seventies can't do the work that would burn up a man half his age," wrote Billy Jr.[1]

He should have known his father better. Hundreds of letters, cards, and telegrams poured in. Farmers, socialites, pastors, former alcoholics—they all offered love and prayers and spoke of the powerful changes in their lives because of Billy Sunday's ministry, inspiring the evangelist to reach more souls for Christ. It was not long before audiences in Millbrook, New York, and Evansville, Indiana, once again heard the old warrior battle for salvation and righteousness.

"Why can't Dad quit and rest the rest of his life? Even working as hard as he does the collections are so small it hardly pays for the strain he has to exert," an exasperated Billy Jr., wrote his mother in May 1935.[2] Perhaps the Sunday brothers should have realized the obvious: One reason Billy hesitated to retire was because of his inability to say no to his children.

Guilt plagued the evangelist. He not only financed George's real estate ventures, Billy Jr.'s dry-ice business, and part of his son-in-law's *Sturgis Journal* building; he continually paid his sons' debts and got them out of

*I wonder if Billy's Nell Sunday
"neglected" their children while
they were "busy" preaching the
Gospel? a sad thought*

scrapes. But George, Billy Jr., and Paul continued to drink, carouse, marry, divorce, and remarry.

George was even wanted by the police, having abused his wives, stolen a rental car, and written bad checks. He was now addicted to morphine. When Nell arrived in Portland, Oregon, to help him and his second wife, Renee, patch up their differences, he beat his wife and commanded his mother to leave. Then he leaped from his fourth-story apartment window. He told Renee at the hospital that he had lost his balance trying to open a stubborn window. Forty-year-old George Sunday died several days later during surgery, less than a year after his sister's death.

"Why, Ma?" Billy mourned. "Why?"

Billy and Nell took little time for regrets. George had left two children, George Jr., and John, whom they loved and promised to support until adulthood. The Sundays built George's first wife, Harriet, a house. George's second wife, Renee, wrote them that she received only seventy-five cents a week from the government: "I know that you would like to forget about me altogether but even with all of that I don't think you would like or let me go hungry."[3] The Sundays sent her a small sum. They rescued Billy Jr., once more when his dry-ice business failed.

Billy's frantic pace kept him focused on saving souls, not lamenting the past. He spoke wherever he could, still jaunty and active in his carefully pressed suits and ties. Billy attacked sin as fearlessly as ever, especially in the clergy. Fellow evangelists such as Aimee Semple McPherson, who faked her own abduction; Sister Smothers, a colorful Tennessee preacher who demonstrated healing powers by handling rattlesnakes; and an Ohio preacher who forgot to obtain divorces before he married multiple wives, all aroused his ire. The changing moral climate, politics, the Depression—they made no difference, as far as God was concerned. Even Billy's personal hurts were not allowed to interfere with the fact that sinners needed to repent and believe in Jesus Christ in order to go to heaven.

To Billy's delight, the gospel message was now being presented on the radio. A fledgling Pittsburgh station, KDKA, had pioneered the first broadcast of a worship service in 1921. Now many ministers spoke over the airwaves, reaching audiences in numbers that took Billy's breath away. He had, at the heyday of his crusade career, preached to crowds of twenty thousand. R. E. Brown, who was called the "Billy Sunday of the air," evangelized five hundred thousand people a week on his radio program. By 1935, several million heard a single broadcast of *The Lutheran Hour*.

No one knew more about attracting crowds than Billy Sunday. He immediately recognized the potential for reaching people who might never enter a church or tabernacle. He even broadcast a few sermons, including one on the *Haven of Rest* program. A New York station invited him to begin a revival series that would attract several million listeners.

Billy and his former choir director, Homer Rodeheaver, had long since reconciled their differences. Now Rody applauded the possible move from live preaching to radio. It might give Billy the opportunity to share the gospel consistently, Rody gently insisted, without spending endless hours in grueling travel, hopping trains, and staying in strange hotels. He and Nell could live in one town, staying close to consistent medical care and making a steady income.

Rody even encouraged Billy to film and distribute some of his sermons, but even as his old friend tried to motivate Billy, he knew the preacher would never adopt such an approach. Billy was and had always been a live performer. He liked big, open halls with platforms and stages, not cramped audio rooms. He loved speaking directly to people; he hated talking to microphones. He wanted to see his listeners cheer, weep, and repent. He cherished the warmth of their hands when they clasped his at the end of a crusade service.

Although Billy's constant traveling exhausted him and damaged his health, he could not bring himself to embrace a more comfortable but less exciting lifestyle. Billy had been a crusade preacher for almost forty years. "I gotta see their eyes, Ma," he told his wife. "Then I know they're on their way to heaven."

Nell understood, so she packed her bags and continued traveling with him, even though she tried to help the seventy-two-year-old evangelist conserve his strength.

Billy suffered another heart attack in Chattanooga in May 1935. His doctors, wife, and family forced him to convalesce for six months in Winona Lake and on his ranch in Oregon. Gradually he regained his strength and visited Billy Jr., and Paul in Los Angeles. He felt much better. The old juices began to flow, the old energy began to bubble, and Billy grew restless.

"I'm tired of sitting around like a helpless, toothless, fat, old lapdog. It's time to get moving again, Ma. There are people out there that need to hear the gospel."

"Billy Sunday," said Nell. "The doctor said you could walk around the block each day a few times. No appointments. No preaching! For once in your life, you are going to listen to him."

Billy glared at her like a stubborn kindergartner, but Nell still could stop him in his tracks when she chose.

Rody drove up, and the two forgot their debate as they greeted him. "I have been directing the music for the Mishawaka First Methodist pastor during his two-week revival," Rody told them as he sipped a cup of coffee. "But I have to go to Washington, D.C., to take care of some business. I wondered if you might want to preach there a night or two, if you're feeling better. It's only fifty to sixty miles away."

"It's less than an hour away," enthused Billy. "I can preach, then come right home, Nell."

Nell gritted her teeth. How could an elderly man turn on that little-boy charm so effectively? "Now, Dad, don't say you'll go. You know the doctor told you that you shouldn't, and you weren't able to."

*"I guess I know how I feel!"*

Billy preached October 25, 1935, in a church whose pews, aisles, platform, and steps were packed full of eager listeners. Some even huddled under the piano. Although gaunt and weak from his heart problems, Billy spoke with some of his old dynamism. The people crowded the building so much that Billy had difficulty conducting his usual altar service at the end. Delighted at the congregation's positive response, Billy agreed to preach the following Sunday afternoon, the last day of the Mishawaka revival.

His eyes glittered with anticipation as they slowly walked up the church steps that rainy October afternoon. Nell noted the crowd was a little smaller. *Maybe it's because of the weather. But I'm glad there's more room.* Billy preached from the book of Acts: " 'Sirs, what must I do to be saved?' And they said, 'Believe on the Lord Jesus Christ and thou shalt be saved, and thy house.' " Forty converts walked to the front to repent of their sins and shake Billy's hand. His face glowed. "Hallelujah! God bless you. The Lord be with you, ma'am."

Nell did not allow Billy to chat until midnight, as he had done in the past. She hustled him into their car and took him home to Winona Lake. "Time to rest," she said firmly, and Billy dropped off in a matter of seconds.

The next morning, the evangelist stayed in bed. He remained weak and tired. "I feel like the power is off," he muttered.[5] Nell called the doctor. Not long after the Mishawaka meeting, Billy recovered enough to travel with Nell to Chicago to take care of some business matters, but on November 6, 1935, he died suddenly at the home of his brother-in-law.

Condolences poured in from factory workers, old friends from Billy's baseball days, bankers, office girls, and government officials. Even President Franklin D. Roosevelt, whose politics Billy had publicly denounced, sent Nell a telegram expressing his sympathy. Christian leaders conducted memorial services in Chicago, Buffalo, and Sioux City, Iowa. Billy was laid to rest in Forest Lawn Cemetery, Chicago, where he had purchased a small plot in 1918.

Billy Sunday's long preaching career changed American revivalism forever. Many had argued that his mass crusade meetings produced few substantial spiritual results. When the evangelist left town, taking his flamboyant rhetoric and acrobatic antics with him, people went back to their old patterns, charged his critics. Some attacked his extreme activism against alcohol. Others criticized his blind patriotism and called him a bigot.

Still others predicted the death of Billy's brand of

Christianity. When 1920s' society rejected Jesus Christ's divinity, death, and resurrection—and the Bible in general—prominent intellectuals declared that soon such naive, barbaric superstition would die with people like Billy Sunday. Within a generation or two, they believed, no one would accept such nonsense.

It did not happen.

Although Billy was dead, a young man still lived who had trembled at hearing Billy's hellfire-and-brimstone message at a 1924 Charlotte, North Carolina, crusade.

His name was Billy Graham.

He would speak at the Winona Lake Bible Conference Center early in his ministry and reach thousands in his huge urban crusades around the world throughout the rest of the century. Although television was a little-known invention during Billy Sunday's lifetime, he would have approved the worldwide broadcasts of enormous, brightly lit stadiums packed with people, the massive choirs singing gospel hymns, and, especially, the wave upon wave of people crowded in front of the platforms where another Billy stood, head bowed in prayer.

He would have heartily amened the principles Graham and other later evangelists integrated into their ministries: complete devotion to preaching the Word, a businesslike approach to crusade planning, and innovation in communicating with people where they were.

He would have laughed to know that by the end of that century, Christianity would be nowhere near its demise, as his enemies had predicted. Forty percent of Americans would lay future claims to heaven because they had confessed their sins and put their personal faith in Jesus Christ.[6] Seventy-three percent would express a belief in the God of the Bible.[7]

Billy Sunday would have laughed, but he would not have been surprised.

After all, God is still God. *amen!*